Everyday Spelling

Practice for Standardized Tests

2

Scott Foresman
Addison Wesley

Editorial Offices: Glenview, Illinois • Menlo Park, California
Sales Offices: Reading, Massachusetts • Duluth, Georgia • Glenview, Illinois
Carrollton, Texas • Menlo Park, California

1-800-552-2259
http://www.sf.aw.com

ISBN 0-673-61811-0

Copyright © 2000
Addison-Wesley Educational Publishers Inc.
All rights reserved.
Printed in the United States of America.

The pages in this book may be duplicated for classroom
use only without further permission from the publisher.

This publication is protected by copyright and permission
should be obtained from the publisher prior to any
prohibited reproduction, storage in a retrieval system, or
transmission in any form or by any means, electronic,
mechanical, photocopying, recording, or otherwise.
For information regarding permission, write to Scott
Foresman-Addison Wesley, 1900 East Lake Avenue,
Glenview, Illinois 60025.

12345678910-PT-0807060504030201 0099

CONTENTS

Lesson Number	Lesson Title	Master Number	Page Number	Answer Page Number
Lesson 1	Writing Enough Letters	1	1	55
Lesson 2	Words with **c**, **k**, and **ck**	2	2	55
Lesson 3	Beginning **br**, **gr**, **st**, **sw**	3	3	55
Lesson 4	Ending **mp**, **nd**, **nt**, **sk**, **st**	4	4	55
Lesson 5	Adding **-s** and **-es**	5	5	56
Lesson 6	Review	6A-6D	6-9	56-57
Lesson 7	**Short e**	7	10	57
Lesson 8	**Short a** and **Short o**	8	11	57
Lesson 9	**Short i** and **Short u**	9	12	57
Lesson 10	Adding **-ed** and **-ing**	10	13	58
Lesson 11	More words with **-ed** and **-ing**	11	14	58
Lesson 12	Review	12A-12D	15-18	58-59
Lesson 13	Using Just Enough Letters	13	19	59
Lesson 14	**Long e**	14	20	59
Lesson 15	**Long a**	15	21	60
Lesson 16	**Long i** and **Long o**	16	22	60
Lesson 17	Vowel Sound in **moon**	17	23	60
Lesson 18	Review	18A-18D	24-27	60-61

Everyday Spelling © Scott Foresman Addison Wesley

CONTENTS

Lesson Number	Lesson Title	Master Number	Page Number	Answer Page Number
Lesson 19	Words with Double Consonants	19	28	61
Lesson 20	Beginning **ch, sh, th, wh**	20	29	62
Lesson 21	Ending **ch, sh, tch, th**	21	30	62
Lesson 22	Words with **ce** and **se**	22	31	62
Lesson 23	Adding **-es**	23	32	62
Lesson 24	Review	24A-24D	33-36	63
Lesson 25	Including All the Letters	25	37	64
Lesson 26	Vowel Sound in **out**	26	38	64
Lesson 27	Vowel Sound with **r**	27	39	64
Lesson 28	More Vowels with **r**	28	40	64
Lesson 29	Words That Sound Alike	29	41	65
Lesson 30	Review	30A-30D	42-45	65-66
Lesson 31	Compound Words	31	46	66
Lesson 32	Contractions	32	47	66
Lesson 33	Vowel Sound in **ball**	33	48	66
Lesson 34	Vowel Sound with **r** and **l**	34	49	67
Lesson 35	Getting Letters in Correct Order	35	50	67
Lesson 36	Review	36A-36D	51-54	67-68

Everyday Spelling © Scott Foresman Addison Wesley

Name _____

LESSON TEST ■ 1

■ Find the word that is spelled correctly to complete each sentence. Fill in the circle to show the correctly spelled word.

Sample:
   I like to ___ the baby.
   (a.) holt   (b.) holed
   ● hold   (d.) hoold

1. It is time for ___ .
   (a.) deb   (b.) bed
   (c.) boad   (d.) beb

2. Please ___ with me.
   (a.) pla   (b.) plae
   (c.) plaee   (d.) play

3. We will ___ a happy song.
   (a.) sing   (b.) sig
   (c.) snig   (d.) sng

4. I have fun at summer ___ .
   (a.) capp   (b.) campe
   (c.) camp   (d.) cammp

5. After winter, comes ___ .
   (a.) sprigh   (b.) spring
   (c.) sring   (d.) sping

6. He will ___ for the toy.
   (a.) pay   (b.) pai
   (c.) piae   (d.) pauee

7. This gift is ___ you.
   (a.) fer   (b.) fo
   (c.) fro   (d.) for

8. Put your ___ on.
   (a.) cap   (b.) caap
   (c.) cep   (d.) caep

9. Lay it ___ on the table.
   (a.) flaat   (b.) flate
   (c.) flet   (d.) flat

10. The new puppies are ___ .
    (a.) fet   (b.) faat
    (c.) fat   (d.) fatt

11. Can you ___ your arm?
    (a.) bend   (b.) bende
    (c.) bened   (d.) benned

12. An army ___ is nearby.
    (a.) forte   (b.) fourt
    (c.) foret   (d.) fort

1

Name _____

2 ■ LESSON TEST

■ Find the word in each group that is spelled correctly. Fill in the circle to show the correctly spelled word.

Sample:
ⓐ sping   ⓑ sring   ● spring   ⓓ srping

1. ⓐ cood   ⓑ coud   ⓒ could   ⓓ coud
2. ⓐ secend   ⓑ second   ⓒ secont   ⓓ secent
3. ⓐ kind   ⓑ cind   ⓒ cine   ⓓ kined
4. ⓐ cen   ⓑ kn   ⓒ kan   ⓓ can
5. ⓐ sik   ⓑ sike   ⓒ sick   ⓓ seke
6. ⓐ woke   ⓑ wolk   ⓒ wook   ⓓ wock
7. ⓐ lik   ⓑ like   ⓒ lk   ⓓ liek
8. ⓐ tooke   ⓑ touck   ⓒ tolk   ⓓ took
9. ⓐ back   ⓑ backe   ⓒ bac   ⓓ bak
10. ⓐ kik   ⓑ kick   ⓒ kicke   ⓓ keik
11. ⓐ pak   ⓑ packe   ⓒ pack   ⓓ pake
12. ⓐ boook   ⓑ booke   ⓒ boock   ⓓ book

Name _____

6A ■ REVIEW TEST

■ Find the word that is spelled correctly to complete each group of words. Fill in the circle on the answer strip to show the correct word.

Sample:
   four, ____, six
   a. fif   b. fiiv
   c. five   d. fiv

ⓐ ⓑ ● ⓓ

1. is ____ in bed
   a. sike   b. sick
   c. sock   d. sik

1. ⓐ ⓑ ⓒ ⓓ

2. girls and ____
   a. boys   b. doys
   c. boyz   d. boyes

2. ⓐ ⓑ ⓒ ⓓ

3. sit at the ____
   a. dask   b. desc
   c. desk   d. desck

3. ⓐ ⓑ ⓒ ⓓ

4. a ____ drawing
   a. grate   b. graet
   c. grat   d. great

4. ⓐ ⓑ ⓒ ⓓ

5. ____ and tigers
   a. lons   b. loins
   c. lions   d. lines

5. ⓐ ⓑ ⓒ ⓓ

6. give you three ____
   a. wishes   b. whishes
   c. wishis   d. wiches

6. ⓐ ⓑ ⓒ ⓓ

7. ____ your bag
   a. packe   b. pack
   c. back   d. pact

7. ⓐ ⓑ ⓒ ⓓ

Everyday Spelling © Scott Foresman Addison Wesley

Name _____

REVIEW TEST ■ 6B

■ Find the word that is spelled correctly to complete each group of words. Fill in the circle on the answer strip to show the correct word.

8. a ____ field
   a. flat   **b.** flatt
   c. falat   **d.** flate

   8. ⓐ ⓑ ⓒ ⓓ

9. she ____ come today
   a. ken   **b.** cane
   c. cen   **d.** can

   9. ⓐ ⓑ ⓒ ⓓ

10. her ____ and sister
    a. brothe   **b.** bruther
    c. brother   **d.** borther

    10. ⓐ ⓑ ⓒ ⓓ

11. candy is ____
    a. sweat   **b.** sweet
    c. swet   **d.** swent

    11. ⓐ ⓑ ⓒ ⓓ

12. a ____ puppy
    a. fatt   **b.** fat
    c. phat   **d.** fate

    12. ⓐ ⓑ ⓒ ⓓ

13. at ____ for the summer
    a. cap   **b.** cape
    c. capp   **d.** camp

    13. ⓐ ⓑ ⓒ ⓓ

14. a farm on the ____
    a. lade   **b.** lad
    c. land   **d.** lamd

    14. ⓐ ⓑ ⓒ ⓓ

Name _____

6C ■ REVIEW TEST

■ Find the word that is spelled correctly to complete each sentence. Fill in the circle on the answer strip to show the correct word.

Sample:
Throw the ___ into the water.   ⓐ ⓑ ● ⓓ
 a. ston   b. stoon
 c. stone   d. stown

15. Will you please ___ this song?   15. ⓐ ⓑ ⓒ ⓓ
 a. sing   b. sung
 c. sinng   d. singing

16. This gift is ___ you.   16. ⓐ ⓑ ⓒ ⓓ
 a. fur   b. four
 c. fore   d. for

17. We had fun in the snow ___.   17. ⓐ ⓑ ⓒ ⓓ
 a. forrt   b. forte
 c. fort   d. fot

18. Kim ___ do it if she tried.   18. ⓐ ⓑ ⓒ ⓓ
 a. koud   b. could
 c. cold   d. cood

19. Dad can sleep days or ___.   19. ⓐ ⓑ ⓒ ⓓ
 a. mights   b. nites
 c. nights   d. nighs

20. She ___ I are ready to go.   20. ⓐ ⓑ ⓒ ⓓ
 a. an   b. in
 c. amd   d. and

21. I ___ my new teacher.   21. ⓐ ⓑ ⓒ ⓓ
 a. like   b. lik
 c. lic   d. liek

Name _____

REVIEW TEST ■ 6D

■ Find the word in each group that is spelled correctly. Fill in the circle on the answer strip to show the correct word.

Sample:
- a. gams
- b. gayms
- c. gaymes
- d. games

ⓐ ⓑ ⓒ ●

22. a. dishish   b. dishes
    c. disice   d. dishez
    22. ⓐ ⓑ ⓒ ⓓ

23. a. grownd   b. groud
    c. ground   d. grond
    23. ⓐ ⓑ ⓒ ⓓ

24. a. difrent   b. differnt
    c. different d. difrint
    24. ⓐ ⓑ ⓒ ⓓ

25. a. brave   b. bave
    c. brav   d. braev
    25. ⓐ ⓑ ⓒ ⓓ

26. a. secent   b. secend
    c. secont   d. second
    26. ⓐ ⓑ ⓒ ⓓ

27. a. jump   b. junp
    c. jummp   d. jupe
    27. ⓐ ⓑ ⓒ ⓓ

28. a. boxez   b. boxes
    c. boxs   d. boxxes
    28. ⓐ ⓑ ⓒ ⓓ

29. a. play   b. pla
    c. plae   d. paly
    29. ⓐ ⓑ ⓒ ⓓ

30. a. baok   b. booke
    c. book   d. boock
    30. ⓐ ⓑ ⓒ ⓓ

Everyday Spelling © Scott Foresman Addison Wesley

Name _____

7 ■ LESSON TEST

■ Find the word that is spelled correctly to complete each sentence. Fill in the circle to show the correctly spelled word.

Sample:
   Put your ____ away.
   ⓐ stuf   ⓑ suff
   ● stuff   ⓓ stof

1. Four ____ are in the car.
   ⓐ menn   ⓑ men
   ⓒ mene   ⓓ meen

2. I do not know ____ to go.
   ⓐ whe   ⓑ wene
   ⓒ whene   ⓓ when

3. He fell and hurt his ____ .
   ⓐ lagg   ⓑ lege
   ⓒ lage   ⓓ leg

4. I see ____ across the street.
   ⓐ thim   ⓑ them
   ⓒ theme   ⓓ tham

5. The dog's nose is ____ .
   ⓐ wet   ⓑ wat
   ⓒ weit   ⓓ weet

6. Please ____ me a dish.
   ⓐ git   ⓑ ge
   ⓒ get   ⓓ gite

7. Let us open our ____ .
   ⓐ presants   ⓑ preasents
   ⓒ presints   ⓓ presents

8. He will not cry ____ it hurts.
   ⓐ unlest   ⓑ unless
   ⓒ unles   ⓓ enless

9. Mom put on her new ____ .
   ⓐ dres   ⓑ drees
   ⓒ dress   ⓓ drass

10. Please, ____ me about it.
    ⓐ tel   ⓑ tell
    ⓒ tal   ⓓ thell

11. I am ____ a new bike.
    ⓐ getting   ⓑ geting
    ⓒ giting   ⓓ gitting

12. He ____ his son help him.
    ⓐ lat   ⓑ let
    ⓒ leted   ⓓ lett

Everyday Spelling © Scott Foresman Addison Wesley

10

Name _____

LESSON TEST ■ 8

■ Find the word in each group that is spelled correctly. Fill in the circle to show the correctly spelled word.

Sample:
    ⓐ itto   ⓑ intoo   ● into   ⓓ itn

1. ⓐ of   ⓑ ov   ⓒ ove   ⓓ uv
2. ⓐ clok   ⓑ clock   ⓒ cloch   ⓓ clook
3. ⓐ sadt   ⓑ sat   ⓒ saet   ⓓ satd
4. ⓐ tha   ⓑ thet   ⓒ that   ⓓ thaet
5. ⓐ rock   ⓑ rok   ⓒ rocke   ⓓ roch
6. ⓐ sadt   ⓑ saad   ⓒ satd   ⓓ sad
7. ⓐ doll   ⓑ dolle   ⓒ dool   ⓓ dooll
8. ⓐ jobb   ⓑ jub   ⓒ job   ⓓ jobe
9. ⓐ bad   ⓑ badt   ⓒ baad   ⓓ batd
10. ⓐ hav   ⓑ haf   ⓒ heve   ⓓ have
11. ⓐ spod   ⓑ spote   ⓒ spot   ⓓ sopt
12. ⓐ vann   ⓑ ven   ⓒ vanne   ⓓ van

Name _____

9 ■ LESSON TEST

■ Find the word that is spelled correctly to complete each sentence. Fill in the circle to show the correctly spelled word.

Sample:
   Rabbits have cute ____ .
   (a.) bunneys   (b.) bunnys
   (c.) bunnis   (●) bunnies

---

1. I will wash, ____ you dry.
   (a.) ef   (b.) if
   (c.) iff   (d.) ife

2. The dog slept on the ____ .
   (a.) rug   (b.) ruge
   (c.) rugg   (d.) rugge

3. What is ____ ?
   (a.) thes   (b.) thise
   (c.) theis   (d.) this

4. It is the right ____ to do.
   (a.) thig   (b.) thing
   (c.) theing   (d.) thaing

5. Jump ____ bed.
   (a.) ento   (b.) intoo
   (c.) in to   (d.) into

6. Our class had an egg ____ .
   (a.) hunt   (b.) hnt
   (c.) hont   (d.) hant

7. The cat blinked ____ eye.
   (a.) it   (b.) its'
   (c.) it's   (d.) its

8. Do not step into the ____ .
   (a.) mud   (b.) mub
   (c.) mude   (d.) mudd

9. The chewing ____ is sweet.
   (a.) gumb   (b.) gome
   (c.) goom   (d.) gum

10. How do those shoes ____ ?
    (a.) fiet   (b.) fidd
    (c.) fit   (d.) fitt

11. Please ____ the door.
    (a.) shud   (b.) shutt
    (c.) shut   (d.) sut

12. Which ____ is on the rose?
    (a.) bugg   (b.) bug
    (c.) buk   (d.) bukk

Name _____

LESSON TEST ■ 10

■ Find the word in each group that is spelled correctly. Fill in the circle to show the correctly spelled word.

Sample:

	● scared	ⓑ skerd	ⓒ skard	ⓓ scard
1.	ⓐ luk	ⓑ looke	ⓒ loock	ⓓ look
2.	ⓐ picked	ⓑ picted	ⓒ pickt	ⓓ pikt
3.	ⓐ walkt	ⓑ wakled	ⓒ walked	ⓓ wakked
4.	ⓐ wot	ⓑ want	ⓒ wat	ⓓ whant
5.	ⓐ lookin	ⓑ loking	ⓒ looking	ⓓ lokeing
6.	ⓐ wonted	ⓑ wanted	ⓒ whanted	ⓓ whated
7.	ⓐ cal	ⓑ coll	ⓒ cail	ⓓ call
8.	ⓐ pick	ⓑ pik	ⓒ pic	ⓓ pikc
9.	ⓐ watching	ⓑ wacthing	ⓒ waching	ⓓ whaching
10.	ⓐ cawling	ⓑ calin	ⓒ calind	ⓓ calling
11.	ⓐ wawk	ⓑ wauk	ⓒ walk	ⓓ waak
12.	ⓐ watch	ⓑ wach	ⓒ whatch	ⓓ wacth

Name _____

11 ■ LESSON TEST

■ Find the word that is spelled correctly to complete each sentence. Fill in the circle to show the correctly spelled word.

Sample:
Eat an ___ in the morning.
ⓐ agg ⓑ eagg
● egg ⓓ eeg

1. I can ___ very fast.
   ⓐ runn ⓑ rn
   ⓒ runne ⓓ run

2. He ___ on the rug.
   ⓐ tript ⓑ triped
   ⓒ tripped ⓓ tripet

3. Give me a big ___ .
   ⓐ huug ⓑ hug
   ⓒ hugg ⓓ hugge

4. Do not ___ that glass!
   ⓐ drop ⓑ dropp
   ⓒ drup ⓓ drep

5. She ___ her mom.
   ⓐ hugged ⓑ hagd
   ⓒ huged ⓓ hugget

6. We will go ___ in the lake.
   ⓐ swmming ⓑ swimming
   ⓒ swming ⓓ swiming

7. The bluebird ___ the worm.
   ⓐ drot ⓑ dropped
   ⓒ droped ⓓ dropt

8. The bus is ___ here.
   ⓐ stoppin ⓑ stupping
   ⓒ stoping ⓓ stopping

9. We are back from our ___ .
   ⓐ trup ⓑ trip
   ⓒ tirp ⓓ tripp

10. He is ___ down the block.
    ⓐ runing ⓑ runnig
    ⓒ runnining ⓓ running

11. Dogs can ___ very well.
    ⓐ swin ⓑ swim
    ⓒ swimm ⓓ swimme

12. Please ___ that now!
    ⓐ stop ⓑ stope
    ⓒ stopp ⓓ stoppe

Name _____

REVIEW TEST ■ 12A

■ Find the word that is spelled correctly to complete each group of words. Fill in the circle on the answer strip to show the correct word.

Sample:
to ___ a dish
a. brack	b. braek
c. break	d. brak

ⓐ ⓑ ● ⓓ

1. walking, and then ___
   a. running	b. runnig
   c. runing	d. rumming

   1. ⓐ ⓑ ⓒ ⓓ

2. took it to ___
   a. then	b. tham
   c. theme	d. them

   2. ⓐ ⓑ ⓒ ⓓ

3. ___ a hot bath
   a. ge	b. get
   c. gat	d. git

   3. ⓐ ⓑ ⓒ ⓓ

4. ___ they all come
   a. when	b. wen
   c. win	d. wene

   4. ⓐ ⓑ ⓒ ⓓ

5. ___ for my sock
   a. hut	b. hont
   c. hunt	d. hant

   5. ⓐ ⓑ ⓒ ⓓ

6. went ___ in the lake
   a. swing	b. swimming
   c. swmming	d. swiming

   6. ⓐ ⓑ ⓒ ⓓ

7. a ___ with six legs
   a. bog	b. bugg
   c. bug	d. bg

   7. ⓐ ⓑ ⓒ ⓓ

Name _____

12B ■ REVIEW TEST

■ Find the word that is spelled correctly to complete each group of words. Fill in the circle on the answer strip to show the correct word.

8. stuck in the ___
   a. mub
   b. mode
   c. mude
   d. mud

   8. ⓐ ⓑ ⓒ ⓓ

9. a ___ and kiss
   a. hugg
   b. huge
   c. hug
   d. hog

   9. ⓐ ⓑ ⓒ ⓓ

10. this one or ___ one
    a. that
    b. thaet
    c. tat
    d. thet

    10. ⓐ ⓑ ⓒ ⓓ

11. can't chew ___
    a. gom
    b. gum
    c. gome
    d. goom

    11. ⓐ ⓑ ⓒ ⓓ

12. take a ___ with her
    a. wake
    b. wock
    c. wak
    d. walk

    12. ⓐ ⓑ ⓒ ⓓ

13. ___ the window
    a. shet
    b. shout
    c. shut
    d. sut

    13. ⓐ ⓑ ⓒ ⓓ

14. ___ I like it
    a. ife
    b. if
    c. i
    d. ef

    14. ⓐ ⓑ ⓒ ⓓ

Name _____

REVIEW TEST ■ 12C

■ Find the word that is spelled correctly to complete each sentence. Fill in the circle on the answer strip to show the correct word.

Sample:
   Come visit ____ as soon as you can.   ⓐ ⓑ ● ⓓ
   a. jost   **b.** gost
   c. just   **d.** jast

---

15. There are ants under the ____.   15. ⓐ ⓑ ⓒ ⓓ
    a. rook   **b.** roch
    c. rack   **d.** rock

16. I ____ a bad cold.   16. ⓐ ⓑ ⓒ ⓓ
    a. have   **b.** hav
    c. half   **d.** haf

17. We all went ____ the school.   17. ⓐ ⓑ ⓒ ⓓ
    a. in two   **b.** into
    c. in to   **d.** intoo

18. Please ____ me a long story.   18. ⓐ ⓑ ⓒ ⓓ
    a. tale   **b.** tall
    c. tell   **d.** till

19. I ____ the large box.   19. ⓐ ⓑ ⓒ ⓓ
    a. want   **b.** wont
    c. what   **d.** whant

20. They ____ in chairs in the room.   20. ⓐ ⓑ ⓒ ⓓ
    a. saet   **b.** sate
    c. set   **d.** sat

21. Last night we ____ a long way.   21. ⓐ ⓑ ⓒ ⓓ
    a. walk   **b.** waked
    c. walkt   **d.** walked

Name _____

12D ■ REVIEW TEST

■ Find the word in each group that is spelled correctly. Fill in the circle on the answer strip to show the correct word.

Sample:
    a. dres   b. drees   ⓐ ⓑ ⓒ ●
    c. drass   d. dress

22. a. droped   b. dropped   22. ⓐ ⓑ ⓒ ⓓ
     c. dropt   d. dopped

23. a. preasents   b. presants   23. ⓐ ⓑ ⓒ ⓓ
     c. presents   d. presints

24. a. swim   b. swin   24. ⓐ ⓑ ⓒ ⓓ
     c. simm   d. swimm

25. a. geting   b. getting   25. ⓐ ⓑ ⓒ ⓓ
     c. giting   d. gitting

26. a. pick   b. pik   26. ⓐ ⓑ ⓒ ⓓ
     c. pikc   d. pic

27. a. wath   b. whatch   27. ⓐ ⓑ ⓒ ⓓ
     c. watch   d. wach

28. a. jobe   b. jub   28. ⓐ ⓑ ⓒ ⓓ
     c. jod   d. job

29. a. sopt   b. spote   29. ⓐ ⓑ ⓒ ⓓ
     c. spot   d. spott

30. a. clock   b. clook   30. ⓐ ⓑ ⓒ ⓓ
     c. cloch   d. clok

Name _____

16 ■ LESSON TEST

■ Find the word that is spelled correctly to complete each sentence. Fill in the circle to show the correctly spelled word.

Sample:
The ____ are wet with rain.
- (a.) stretes
- ● streets
- (c.) streats
- (d.) srtets

---

1. I can ____ you a trick.
   - (a.) showe
   - (b.) seou
   - (c.) sowe
   - (d.) show

2. We live ____ on a hill.
   - (a.) hight
   - (b.) hie
   - (c.) high
   - (d.) hiy

3. Step into the ____ slowly.
   - (a.) bote
   - (b.) boute
   - (c.) boat
   - (d.) baot

4. Do your work the ____ way.
   - (a.) right
   - (b.) righth
   - (c.) ritte
   - (d.) rihgt

5. I do not ____ if you do not.
   - (a.) minde
   - (b.) miad
   - (c.) minte
   - (d.) mind

6. Will you ____ me the ball?
   - (a.) trow
   - (b.) throw
   - (c.) traw
   - (d.) thro

7. My duck can ____ in the tub.
   - (a.) floote
   - (b.) float
   - (c.) flaut
   - (d.) floot

8. I saw a ____ on the farm.
   - (a.) goat
   - (b.) goot
   - (c.) gaot
   - (d.) gote

9. Turn on the ____ please.
   - (a.) lith
   - (b.) lihgt
   - (c.) light
   - (d.) ligth

10. This is my ____ pencil.
    - (a.) owen
    - (b.) owne
    - (c.) oun
    - (d.) own

11. Can you ____ where I hid it?
    - (a.) finde
    - (b.) find
    - (c.) feind
    - (d.) fiend

12. We all go home at ____ .
    - (a.) nighe
    - (b.) nite
    - (c.) nigth
    - (d.) night

Name _____

LESSON TEST ■ 17

■ Find the word in each group that is spelled correctly. Fill in the circle to show the correctly spelled word.

Sample:
  (a) lunshes   (b) lunchs   ● lunches   (d) lunshs

1. (a) teu   (b) too   (c) towe   (d) towo
2. (a) chew   (b) cheu   (c) chue   (d) chooe
3. (a) room   (b) rume   (c) roun   (d) romme
4. (a) mon   (b) moon   (c) mone   (d) meun
5. (a) fod   (b) fode   (c) fowd   (d) food
6. (a) new   (b) nue   (c) newe   (d) nuw
7. (a) gorwed   (b) groo   (c) gru   (d) grew
8. (a) zeu   (b) zew   (c) zoo   (d) zo
9. (a) blogh   (b) blu   (c) blew   (d) bloew
10. (a) sone   (b) soon   (c) seun   (d) soone
11. (a) fluew   (b) flwe   (c) fliw   (d) flew
12. (a) knew   (b) kenew   (c) noew   (d) neuw

Name _____

18A ■ REVIEW TEST

■ Find the group of words in which the underlined word is misspelled. Fill in the circle on the answer strip to show that group of words.

Sample:
  a. <u>leaves</u> on the tree
  b. a <u>graet</u> big kiss
  c. <u>when</u> the bus comes
  d. a <u>sweet</u>, juicy apple

  1. ⓐ ● ⓒ ⓓ

1. a. open or <u>shut</u>
   b. letters and other <u>mayel</u>
   c. the best <u>thing</u> to do
   d. <u>across</u> the wide street

   1. ⓐ ⓑ ⓒ ⓓ

2. a. <u>swims</u> like a fish
   b. <u>between</u> you and me
   c. the <u>rite</u> thing to do
   d. to <u>follow</u> the leader

   2. ⓐ ⓑ ⓒ ⓓ

3. a. <u>flat</u> on his back
   b. looked at the <u>clock</u>
   c. <u>flue</u> the kite today
   d. sat on the <u>ground</u>

   3. ⓐ ⓑ ⓒ ⓓ

4. a. to ship the big <u>boxes</u>
   b. take it <u>away</u> from here
   c. big <u>bump</u> on the head
   d. <u>allways</u> do a good job

   4. ⓐ ⓑ ⓒ ⓓ

5. a. <u>red</u> me the book
   b. my <u>brother</u> and sister
   c. a <u>truck</u> or a van
   d. the <u>families</u> are going

   5. ⓐ ⓑ ⓒ ⓓ

6. a. a <u>bend</u> in the road
   b. <u>livd</u> on a little farm
   c. camping out at <u>night</u>
   d. will <u>check</u> the papers

   6. ⓐ ⓑ ⓒ ⓓ

7. a. sat on wet <u>paite</u>
   b. to <u>push</u> the cart
   c. not <u>much</u> money
   d. <u>getting</u> ready to go

   7. ⓐ ⓑ ⓒ ⓓ

Name _____

REVIEW TEST ■ 18B

■ Find the group of words in which the underlined word is misspelled. Fill in the circle on the answer strip to show that group of words.

8. **a.** <u>played</u> with the boys
   b. <u>mud</u> on our shoes
   c. <u>trip</u> on the old rug
   d. on the <u>teem</u> that won

   8. (a) (b) (c) (d)

9. **a.** <u>aet</u> a big meal
   b. did not <u>fit</u> well
   c. <u>grew</u> a few inches
   d. <u>swimming</u> very far

   9. (a) (b) (c) (d)

10. **a.** <u>running</u> up the road
    b. <u>dropped</u> in the snow
    c. will leave very <u>son</u>
    d. a <u>Halloween</u> <u>party</u>

    10. (a) (b) (c) (d)

11. **a.** will go my <u>way</u>
    b. <u>fowd</u> on the table
    c. <u>because</u> they want
    d. <u>have</u> a green car

    11. (a) (b) (c) (d)

12. **a.** <u>dishes</u> in the sink
    b. <u>blew</u> a large bubble
    c. a <u>clock</u> with no hands
    d. no shoes on her <u>feat</u>

    12. (a) (b) (c) (d)

13. **a.** clean, white <u>teeth</u>
    b. a <u>bout</u> on the lake
    c. ride three <u>ponies</u>
    d. <u>hugged</u> her child

    13. (a) (b) (c) (d)

14. **a.** <u>mak</u> a large box
    b. out in the <u>rain</u>
    c. <u>until</u> the next day
    d. a stick of <u>gum</u>

    14. (a) (b) (c) (d)

Everyday Spelling © Scott Foresman Addison Wesley

Name _____

18C ■ REVIEW TEST

■ Find the word that is spelled correctly to complete each sentence. Fill in the circle on the answer strip to show the correct word.

Sample:
We were ___ TV.
a. waching b. whaching
c. watching d. wacthing

ⓐ ⓑ ● ⓓ

15. I have a ___ toy.
a. now b. mew
c. new d. knew

15. ⓐ ⓑ ⓒ ⓓ

16. Please ___ me the ball.
a. thore b. thow
c. through d. throw

16. ⓐ ⓑ ⓒ ⓓ

17. The jet is ___ in the air.
a. hie b. hight
c. hi d. high

17. ⓐ ⓑ ⓒ ⓓ

18. I like you ___.
a. a lot b. allot
c. alot d. alote

18. ⓐ ⓑ ⓒ ⓓ

19. Did you ___ your pencil?
a. fied b. fined
c. find d. finde

19. ⓐ ⓑ ⓒ ⓓ

20. You can ___ how cold my hands are.
a. feal b. feel
c. fell d. fill

20. ⓐ ⓑ ⓒ ⓓ

21. She has made up her ___ to go.
a. mide b. mine
c. mind d. minde

21. ⓐ ⓑ ⓒ ⓓ

Name _____

REVIEW TEST ■ 18D

■ Find the word in each group that is spelled correctly. Fill in the circle on the answer strip to show the correct word.

Sample:
a. ef   b. iff   ⓐ ⓑ ⓒ ●
c. ife   d. if

---

22. a. scared   b. scard   22. ⓐ ⓑ ⓒ ⓓ
    c. skerd   d. skard

23. a. a pone   b. apon   23. ⓐ ⓑ ⓒ ⓓ
    c. opon   d. upon

24. a. basball   b. baceball 24. ⓐ ⓑ ⓒ ⓓ
    c. baseball d. base ball

25. a. stay   b. sta   25. ⓐ ⓑ ⓒ ⓓ
    c. saty   d. stae

26. a. cep   b. keep   26. ⓐ ⓑ ⓒ ⓓ
    c. kep   d. ceep

27. a. ech   b. each   27. ⓐ ⓑ ⓒ ⓓ
    c. eatch   d. eche

28. a. mun   b. muon   28. ⓐ ⓑ ⓒ ⓓ
    c. mone   d. moon

29. a. gowing   b. goning   29. ⓐ ⓑ ⓒ ⓓ
    c. going   d. goin

30. a. was   b. wase   30. ⓐ ⓑ ⓒ ⓓ
    c. wus   d. wos

Name _____

19 ■ LESSON TEST

■ Find the word in each group that is spelled correctly. Fill in the circle to show the correctly spelled word.

Sample:

ⓐ wat   ⓑ wate   ⓒ wath   ● what

1. ⓐ happe   ⓑ happy   ⓒ hapey   ⓓ happey
2. ⓐ pritty   ⓑ pretty   ⓒ prity   ⓓ prety
3. ⓐ eg   ⓑ eeg   ⓒ egg   ⓓ agg
4. ⓐ tall   ⓑ tawl   ⓒ tal   ⓓ taul
5. ⓐ betur   ⓑ better   ⓒ beder   ⓓ beter
6. ⓐ ful   ⓑ foll   ⓒ fole   ⓓ full
7. ⓐ cary   ⓑ carry   ⓒ carrye   ⓓ carrey
8. ⓐ follow   ⓑ follo   ⓒ folow   ⓓ folo
9. ⓐ stuff   ⓑ stuf   ⓒ stof   ⓓ stofe
10. ⓐ halloween ⓑ holloween ⓒ Halloween   ⓓ hallween
11. ⓐ wil   ⓑ wel   ⓒ whill   ⓓ will
12. ⓐ atd   ⓑ att   ⓒ add   ⓓ adt

Name _____

LESSON TEST ■ 20

■ Find the word that is spelled correctly to complete each sentence. Fill in the circle to show the correctly spelled word.

Sample:
Did you ___ the glass?
(a.) brack   (b.) braek
(c.) brak   ● break

1. Button your ___ .
   (a.) shirt   (b.) shert
   (c.) shrit   (d.) shurt

2. That ___ is broken.
   (a.) chare   (b.) chir
   (c.) chair   (d.) chiar

3. Where is ___ cat?
   (a.) tha   (b.) the
   (c.) teh   (d.) th

4. Are ___ too many?
   (a.) thar   (b.) thair
   (c.) thier   (d.) there

5. I know ___ I will do.
   (a.) waht   (b.) wat
   (c.) wut   (d.) what

6. He will ___ his work.
   (a.) cheack   (b.) check
   (c.) chec   (d.) chech

7. Please finish; ___ clean up.
   (a.) then   (b.) thene
   (c.) tehn   (d.) theen

8. I wonder ___ Mom went.
   (a.) wer   (b.) whare
   (c.) where   (d.) wher

9. The dog is brown and ___ .
   (a.) white   (b.) wite
   (c.) wight   (d.) whit

10. We must ___ the package.
    (a.) shep   (b.) ship
    (c.) shipp   (d.) shipe

11. What a good ___ she is!
    (a.) child   (b.) chid
    (c.) childe   (d.) ciled

12. We will eat when ___ arrive.
    (a.) thay   (b.) tha
    (c.) thae   (d.) they

Name _____

21 ■ LESSON TEST

■ Find the word in each group that is spelled correctly. Fill in the circle to show the correctly spelled word.

Sample:

(a) aske   (b) asge   ● ask   (d) asak

1. (a) bath   (b) baath   (c) batth   (d) bothe
2. (a) warsh   (b) waush   (c) wash   (d) wost
3. (a) wich   (b) which   (c) whitch   (d) wicth
4. (a) inch   (b) intch   (c) ench   (d) insh
5. (a) crash   (b) crach   (c) cratsh   (d) chrash
6. (a) cach   (b) catch   (c) cacth   (d) cech
7. (a) whith   (b) weth   (c) with   (d) wiht
8. (a) puch   (b) pusch   (c) puhs   (d) push
9. (a) mutch   (b) much   (c) moch   (d) musch
10. (a) reach (b) reech   (c) reesh   (d) reatch
11. (a) bolth (b) bouth   (c) bothe   (d) both
12. (a) pich   (b) pitch   (c) pictch   (d) pithch

Everyday Spelling © Scott Foresman Addison Wesley

Name _____

LESSON TEST ■ 22

■ Find the word that is spelled correctly to complete each sentence. Fill in the circle to show the correctly spelled word.

Sample:
   She has a wonderful ___ .
   (a.) frend   (●) friend
   (c.) frind   (d.) freind

1. The ___ has a new colt.
   (a.) horse   (b.) hores
   (c.) hourse   (d.) hors

2. Which of ___ is yours?
   (a.) thos   (b.) those
   (c.) thoes   (d.) thoses

3. The park is a pretty ___ .
   (a.) plase   (b.) plas
   (c.) plaes   (d.) place

4. Do ___ belong to her?
   (a.) these   (b.) thes
   (c.) theese   (d.) thees

5. It is very ___ of you.
   (a.) nis   (b.) nic
   (c.) nise   (d.) nice

6. Will you ___ help?
   (a.) plese   (b.) please
   (c.) pleas   (d.) ples

7. We live in a brick ___ .
   (a.) hows   (b.) house
   (c.) houes   (d.) hous

8. He swims ___ a week.
   (a.) wuns   (b.) onec
   (c.) once   (d.) wonce

9. It is ___ it is hot.
   (a.) becouse   (b.) becuse
   (c.) becase   (d.) because

10. She hopes to win the ___ .
    (a.) ras   (b.) race
    (c.) raes   (d.) rase

11. Can you ___ this crayon?
    (a.) yoos   (b.) uooz
    (c.) use   (d.) uese

12. I hear ___ music.
    (a.) dans   (b.) dace
    (c.) danc   (d.) dance

Name _____

23 ■ LESSON TEST

■ Find the word in each group that is spelled correctly. Fill in the circle to show the correctly spelled word.

Sample:
 (a) thim ● them (c) tham (d) thum

1. (a) poney (b) pony (c) ponie (d) ponny
2. (a) baby (b) babay (c) babey (d) babby
3. (a) storyies (b) storys (c) stroys (d) stories
4. (a) family (b) famly (c) faimly (d) famaly
5. (a) pupes (b) puppies (c) pupies (d) puppys
6. (a) babys (b) babies (c) babyes (d) babbies
7. (a) pupy (b) pupey (c) puppy (d) puppie
8. (a) poneys (b) ponys (c) ponneys (d) ponies
9. (a) bunneys (b) bunnies (c) bunnys (d) bunnis
10. (a) families (b) familys (c) famlies (d) familyes
11. (a) storey (b) storie (c) story (d) storee
12. (a) bunny (b) bunee (c) buny (d) bunney

32

Name _____

REVIEW TEST ■ 24A

■ Find the group of words in which the underlined word is misspelled. Fill in the circle on the answer strip to show that group of words.

Sample:
   a. <u>could</u> not see it
   b. to <u>asge</u> for help
   c. days and <u>nights</u>
   d. <u>wishes</u> for a dog

ⓐ ● ⓒ ⓓ

1. a. <u>cap</u> on his head
   b. <u>dishes</u> on the table
   c. <u>went</u> to a show
   d. <u>wight</u> sheet of paper

1. ⓐ ⓑ ⓒ ⓓ

2. a. went there <u>ounce</u>
   b. to put into <u>boxes</u>
   c. <u>bump</u> on his leg
   d. to <u>play</u> the game

2. ⓐ ⓑ ⓒ ⓓ

3. a. took a <u>walk</u>
   b. to <u>pay</u> for the toy
   c. sit on a <u>char</u>
   d. <u>pack</u> of wolves

3. ⓐ ⓑ ⓒ ⓓ

4. a. marks an <u>ench</u> apart
   b. <u>brother</u> and sister
   c. to <u>sing</u> a song
   d. will <u>jump</u> up and down

4. ⓐ ⓑ ⓒ ⓓ

5. a. pages in a <u>book</u>
   b. take a hot <u>bathe</u>
   c. <u>must</u> come home now
   d. <u>different</u> from this one

5. ⓐ ⓑ ⓒ ⓓ

6. a. in your <u>desk</u>
   b. my home <u>state</u>
   c. are <u>thay</u> coming
   d. to <u>land</u> on the floor

6. ⓐ ⓑ ⓒ ⓓ

7. a. go to the <u>dance</u>
   b. <u>lions</u> and tigers
   c. to <u>add</u> and subtract
   d. a loud <u>chrash</u> outside

7. ⓐ ⓑ ⓒ ⓓ

Name _____

24B ■ REVIEW TEST

■ Find the group of words in which the underlined word is misspelled. Fill in the circle on the answer strip to show that group of words.

8. a. <u>for</u> you and me
   b. two ripe <u>apples</u>
   c. ducks and <u>bunnys</u>
   d. <u>add</u> these up

   8. ⓐ ⓑ ⓒ ⓓ

9. a. to <u>bend</u> down
   b. <u>follo</u> a girl in front
   c. just <u>like</u> you
   d. three <u>nights</u> ago

   9. ⓐ ⓑ ⓒ ⓓ

10. a. will <u>carry</u> it for you
    b. to <u>reach</u> up for it
    c. has a good <u>use</u>
    d. <u>cheack</u> all his work

    10. ⓐ ⓑ ⓒ ⓓ

11. a. six in my <u>famly</u>
    b. a good <u>book</u>
    c. a <u>spot</u> on his car
    d. to <u>kick</u> it hard

    11. ⓐ ⓑ ⓒ ⓓ

12. a. each of <u>they</u> books
    b. to <u>swing</u> back and forth
    c. <u>stand</u> next to
    d. down on hard <u>ground</u>

    12. ⓐ ⓑ ⓒ ⓓ

13. a. to <u>let</u> him go
    b. to <u>catch</u> a fish
    c. mother, father, and <u>ciled</u>
    d. play in a <u>fort</u>

    13. ⓐ ⓑ ⓒ ⓓ

14. a. give you three <u>wishes</u>
    b. <u>boys</u> in a game
    c. has been very <u>sick</u>
    d. hear <u>storys</u> at bedtime

    14. ⓐ ⓑ ⓒ ⓓ

Name _____

26 ■ LESSON TEST

■ Find the word in each group that is spelled correctly. Fill in the circle to show the correctly spelled word.

Sample:
- (a) pithch
- (b) pictch
- (c) pich
- ● pitch

1. (a) toun (b) twon (c) town (d) tonw
2. (a) about (b) abot (c) a bout (d) abowt
3. (a) aut (b) out (c) ot (d) owt
4. (a) owr (b) ar (c) oure (d) our
5. (a) nauw (b) naw (c) now (d) noe
6. (a) found (b) founed (c) fownd (d) founde
7. (a) maus (b) mouse (c) mause (d) mous
8. (a) doun (b) down (c) daun (d) downe
9. (a) roud (b) rownd (c) roand (d) round
10. (a) hou (b) haw (c) howe (d) how
11. (a) klown (b) clown (c) klaun (d) claun
12. (a) sound (b) sond (c) sownd (d) sowd

Name _____

LESSON TEST ■ 27

■ Find the word that is spelled correctly to complete each sentence. Fill in the circle to show the correctly spelled word.

Sample:
   I once rode a big ___.
   ● horse   (b.) hores
   (c.) hors   (d.) hourse

1. How ___ away do you live?
   (a.) fure   (b.) farre
   (c.) firr   (d.) far

2. It is ___ to learn to swim.
   (a.) hord   (b.) hard
   (c.) harb   (d.) harde

3. We had a ___ for Dad.
   (a.) pardy   (b.) party
   (c.) partey (d.) partty

4. His dog has a loud ___.
   (a.) bark   (b.) barck
   (c.) brck   (d.) brok

5. It gets ___ after 5:00.
   (a.) darke   (b.) drack
   (c.) dark   (d.) darck

6. I would like to visit a ___.
   (a.) farn   (b.) fram
   (c.) furm   (d.) farm

7. Pull your sister in the ___.
   (a.) carte   (b.) crt
   (c.) cart   (d.) carde

8. We saw the band ___.
   (a.) mardsh (b.) mardch
   (c.) martch (d.) march

9. She has a cut on her ___.
   (a.) aurt   (b.) arm
   (c.) aerm   (d.) aurm

10. What ___ do you play?
    (a.) part   (b.) prt
    (c.) purt   (d.) parte

11. The cows are in the ___.
    (a.) barn   (b.) barne
    (c.) barrn   (d.) brn

12. We ___ without you.
    (a.) strated (b.) starded
    (c.) started (d.) startid

Name _____

28 ■ LESSON TEST

■ Find the word in each group that is spelled correctly. Fill in the circle to show the correctly spelled word.

Sample:
- ● lion (b) lyon (c) leon (d) lyen

1. (a) first (b) frist (c) ferst (d) firt
2. (a) bern (b) birn (c) burne (d) burn
3. (a) hert (b) hurt (c) hirt (d) herte
4. (a) lern (b) learn (c) learne (d) larn
5. (a) prson (b) prsen (c) person (d) persen
6. (a) garl (b) grle (c) gril (d) girl
7. (a) har (b) her (c) hre (d) hr
8. (a) were (b) weare (c) woer (d) wer
9. (a) turne (b) tirn (c) tirne (d) turn
10. (a) haerd (b) hurd (c) heerd (d) heard
11. (a) turtel (b) turtle (c) trutle (d) turttl
12. (a) bird (b) burd (c) bured (d) bired

Name _____

LESSON TEST ■ 29

■ Find the word that is spelled correctly to complete each sentence. Fill in the circle to show the correctly spelled word.

Sample:
   May I have ____ one more?
   (a.) jost   (b.) gost
   (c.) jus   ● just

1. I can do it ____ myself.
   (a.) bey   (b.) bie
   (c.) biy   (d.) by

2. We are all ____ now.
   (a.) hir   (b.) herre
   (c.) here   (d.) heare

3. He has gone ____ see her.
   (a.) towe   (b.) tu
   (c.) to   (d.) ta

4. Do you ____ the way?
   (a.) know   (b.) nowe
   (c.) noew   (d.) noo

5. Close one ____ at a time.
   (a.) eey   (b.) eye
   (c.) ei   (d.) eaye

6. Our ____ cousins are here.
   (a.) tuo   (b.) two
   (c.) tu   (d.) taw

7. At last, I have ____!
   (a.) wone   (b.) wun
   (c.) won   (d.) whon

8. Do you ____ the music?
   (a.) heer   (b.) heare
   (c.) hir   (d.) hear

9. I think Mom said ____.
   (a.) noo   (b.) mo
   (c.) no   (d.) nao

10. ____ think it is Tuesday.
    (a.) Y   (b.) I
    (c.) Ey   (d.) i

11. I would like to ____ a book.
    (a.) buy   (b.) bey
    (c.) bai   (d.) bie

12. Which ____ would you like?
    (a.) wun   (b.) one
    (c.) whone   (d.) wan

Everyday Spelling © Scott Foresman Addison Wesley

Name _____

30A ■ REVIEW TEST

■ Find the word that is spelled correctly to complete each group of words. Fill in the circle on the answer strip to show the correct word.

Sample:
____ up at 7 o'clock   ⓐ ⓑ ● ⓓ
a. whok   b. wook
c. woke   d. wock

1. ____ thing or another   1. ⓐ ⓑ ⓒ ⓓ
   a. wone   b. on
   c. one   d. won

2. a ____ dark sky   2. ⓐ ⓑ ⓒ ⓓ
   a. very   b. vary
   c. verry   d. vere

3. saw it ____ the window   3. ⓐ ⓑ ⓒ ⓓ
   a. trough   b. threw
   c. throw   d. through

4. people in the ____   4. ⓐ ⓑ ⓒ ⓓ
   a. twon   b. town
   c. ton   d. toun

5. showed her ____ to ride the bike   5. ⓐ ⓑ ⓒ ⓓ
   a. how   b. haw
   c. hou   d. who

6. money to ____ the food   6. ⓐ ⓑ ⓒ ⓓ
   a. bey   b. by
   c. buy   d. bye

7. get there ____ I do   7. ⓐ ⓑ ⓒ ⓓ
   a. be for   b. befour
   c. befor   d. before

Name _____

REVIEW TEST ■ 30B

■ Find the word that is spelled correctly to complete each group of words. Fill in the circle on the answer strip to show the correct word.

8. fell ___ on the rug
   a. doun
   b. down
   c. bown
   d. don

8. ⓐ ⓑ ⓒ ⓓ

9. rock ___ the tall tree
   a. dy
   b. by
   c. buy
   d. biy

9. ⓐ ⓑ ⓒ ⓓ

10. ___ or three children
    a. two
    b. to
    c. too
    d. tow

10. ⓐ ⓑ ⓒ ⓓ

11. took the ___ bag
    a. wole
    b. holl
    c. hole
    d. whole

11. ⓐ ⓑ ⓒ ⓓ

12. felt the ___ bump
    a. hrd
    b. heard
    c. hard
    d. hod

12. ⓐ ⓑ ⓒ ⓓ

13. ___ how to do it
    a. know
    b. kow
    c. no
    d. now

13. ⓐ ⓑ ⓒ ⓓ

14. team ___ the big game
    a. one
    b. won
    c. wun
    d. wone

14. ⓐ ⓑ ⓒ ⓓ

Name _____

30C ■ REVIEW TEST

■ Find the word that is spelled correctly to complete each sentence. Fill in the circle on the answer strip to show the correct word.

Sample:
Tell him ____ one you want.   ⓐ ⓑ ● ⓓ
   a. wich   b. whitch
   c. which   d. wiche

15. Please come ____ my magic show.   15. ⓐ ⓑ ⓒ ⓓ
   a. tow   b. too
   c. two   d. to

16. Every child has a ____ in the play.   16. ⓐ ⓑ ⓒ ⓓ
   a. part   b. port
   c. prt   d. prat

17. I need ____ paper.   17. ⓐ ⓑ ⓒ ⓓ
   a. som   b. same
   c. some   d. sum

18. She can tell that you ____ late.   18. ⓐ ⓑ ⓒ ⓓ
   a. were   b. wher
   c. where   d. wer

19. I ____ like a fresh orange.   19. ⓐ ⓑ ⓒ ⓓ
   a. woud   b. wold
   c. would   d. wood

20. He ____ to race fast.   20. ⓐ ⓑ ⓒ ⓓ
   a. stated   b. started
   c. starded   d. stared

21. You will get ____ more candy!   21. ⓐ ⓑ ⓒ ⓓ
   a. on   b. now
   c. know   d. no

Name _____

REVIEW TEST ■ 30D

■ Find the word in each group that is spelled correctly. Fill in the circle on the answer strip to show the correct word.

Sample:
    a. acros   **b.** acrost   ⓐ ⓑ ⓒ ●
    c. accross   **d.** across

22. **a.** favorite   **b.** favrit   22. ⓐ ⓑ ⓒ ⓓ
    c. favrite   **d.** favorit

23. **a.** prson   **b.** peson   23. ⓐ ⓑ ⓒ ⓓ
    c. persen   **d.** person

24. **a.** owt   **b.** aut   24. ⓐ ⓑ ⓒ ⓓ
    c. out   **d.** ot

25. **a.** a bout   **b.** abot   25. ⓐ ⓑ ⓒ ⓓ
    c. abowt   **d.** about

26. **a.** sowd   **b.** sound   26. ⓐ ⓑ ⓒ ⓓ
    c. sownd   **d.** sond

27. **a.** bark   **b.** berk   27. ⓐ ⓑ ⓒ ⓓ
    c. brok   **d.** barck

28. **a.** ya   **b.** you   28. ⓐ ⓑ ⓒ ⓓ
    c. u   **d.** yo

29. **a.** frst   **b.** firt   29. ⓐ ⓑ ⓒ ⓓ
    c. frist   **d.** first

30. **a.** evrey   **b.** evry   30. ⓐ ⓑ ⓒ ⓓ
    c. every   **d.** evey

Name _____

31 ■ LESSON TEST

■ Find the word in each group that is spelled correctly. Fill in the circle to show the correctly spelled word.

Sample:
    ⓐ gote   ⓑ gaot   ⓒ goot   ● goat

1. ⓐ some thing   ⓑ something   ⓒ somthing   ⓓ somting
2. ⓐ birtday   ⓑ birthday   ⓒ birth day   ⓓ berthday
3. ⓐ bathtup   ⓑ bafftub   ⓒ bathtube   ⓓ bathtub
4. ⓐ somthines   ⓑ somtimes   ⓒ sometimes   ⓓ some times
5. ⓐ air plane   ⓑ airplane   ⓒ airplain   ⓓ ariplane
6. ⓐ everthing   ⓑ everything   ⓒ every thing   ⓓ evrething
7. ⓐ outside   ⓑ outsied   ⓒ out sid   ⓓ out side
8. ⓐ everybody   ⓑ eavrybody   ⓒ every body   ⓓ everbody
9. ⓐ sun chine   ⓑ sonshine   ⓒ sunshine   ⓓ sun shin
10. ⓐ playground   ⓑ play ground   ⓒ playgrownd   ⓓ playgrowd
11. ⓐ my self   ⓑ myselfe   ⓒ myself   ⓓ myslef
12. ⓐ inside   ⓑ insid   ⓒ in cide   ⓓ innside

Name _____

LESSON TEST ■ 32

■ Find the word that is spelled correctly to complete each sentence. Fill in the circle to show the correctly spelled word.

Sample:
   I like to ___ TV at 7:00.
   ⓐ wach   ● watch
   ⓒ wacth   ⓓ whatch

1. He thought I ___ see him.
   ⓐ din't   ⓑ didn't
   ⓒ dident   ⓓ didnt

2. Why ___ he home yet?
   ⓐ isnt   ⓑ is'nt
   ⓒ isen't   ⓓ isn't

3. Mom said ___ one for you.
   ⓐ ders   ⓑ there's
   ⓒ thers   ⓓ ther's

4. Oh, ___ the one I wanted!
   ⓐ here's   ⓑ heares
   ⓒ heres   ⓓ heers

5. I think ___ mine.
   ⓐ thats   ⓑ thatts
   ⓒ that's   ⓓ thas

6. Do you know if ___ ready?
   ⓐ its   ⓑ itss
   ⓒ it's   ⓓ i'ts

7. I hope ___ not the last one.
   ⓐ Im   ⓑ i'm
   ⓒ Ime   ⓓ I'm

8. I ___ want to do that.
   ⓐ don't   ⓑ downt
   ⓒ dont   ⓓ dount

9. They said ___ ready to start.
   ⓐ ther   ⓑ thar
   ⓒ the're   ⓓ they're

10. Are you sure you ___ do it?
    ⓐ con't   ⓑ can't
    ⓒ kant   ⓓ cant

11. She ___ the first to finish.
    ⓐ wasen't   ⓑ wasn't
    ⓒ wasent   ⓓ was'nt

12. Now ___ on our way.
    ⓐ wer   ⓑ weer
    ⓒ we're   ⓓ we'r

Name _____

33 ■ LESSON TEST

■ Find the word in each group that is spelled correctly. Fill in the circle to show the correctly spelled word.

Sample:
    (a) realy   (b) relly   ● really   (d) rilly

1. (a) crawl   (b) craul   (c) crael   (d) crawal
2. (a) smal   (b) smol   (c) samll   (d) small
3. (a) hawl   (b) haule   (c) hall   (d) halle
4. (a) aweful   (b) awfull   (c) awful   (d) aful
5. (a) bole   (b) ball   (c) bawle   (d) bal
6. (a) fall   (b) fawl   (c) fal   (d) flol
7. (a) bougth   (b) bot   (c) boaught   (d) bought
8. (a) brouth   (b) brot   (c) brought   (d) broght
9. (a) saw   (b) sall   (c) sawe   (d) sowe
10. (a) ole   (b) al   (c) ol   (d) all
11. (a) thout   (b) thought   (c) thot   (d) thaught
12. (a) drawe   (b) draw   (c) dra   (d) dray

Name _____

LESSON TEST ■ 34

■ Find the word that is spelled correctly to complete each sentence. Fill in the circle to show the correctly spelled word.

Sample:
The boys ___ home together.
● went   b. wint
c. whent   d. wen

1. Do you have a ___ crayon?
   a. purple   b. perple
   c. purpl   d. purpul

2. Pick a shirt of ___ color.
   a. a nother   b. anouther
   c. another   d. anather

3. I bit into a sweet ___ .
   a. appel   b. appl
   c. apple   d. appal

4. She brushes ___ eating.
   a. afther   b. afeter
   c. aftr   d. after

5. Will he ___ get here?
   a. evere   b. ever
   c. aver   d. evr

6. The glass rolled off the ___ .
   a. tabel   b. table
   c. tabble   d. tabule

7. There are 30 ___ in here.
   a. peaple   b. peple
   c. people   d. peapul

8. Should I do it ___ again?
   a. over   b. ovre
   c. ovr   d. overe

9. What is ___ your chair?
   a. ander   b. undere
   c. onder   d. under

10. It's a pretty ___ song.
    a. littel   b. litte
    c. little   d. littl

11. Take one or the ___ .
    a. other   b. ather
    c. outher   d. otheer

12. Put the ___ into the vase.
    a. flowr   b. flowre
    c. flawr   d. flower

Name _____

35 ■ LESSON TEST

■ Find the word in each group that is spelled correctly. Fill in the circle to show the correctly spelled word.

Sample:
- ● march (b) martch (c) mardch (d) mardsh

1. (a) tried (b) tride (c) treid (d) tryed
2. (a) specil (b) special (c) speical (d) speshel
3. (a) gouse (b) gose (c) goes (d) gos
4. (a) agen (b) agin (c) again (d) agian
5. (a) cildren (b) chillren (c) childeren (d) children
6. (a) ho (b) who (c) whoe (d) whoo
7. (a) said (b) sead (c) siad (d) sed
8. (a) caht (b) caught (c) cought (d) cauht
9. (a) frends (b) friends (c) freinds (d) frens
10. (a) beatiful (b) beautifull (c) beutiful (d) beautiful
11. (a) aint (b) ont (c) aunt (d) awnt
12. (a) Chrishmas (b) christmas (c) Chrismas (d) Christmas

Name _____

36D ■ REVIEW TEST

■ Find the word in each group that is spelled correctly. Fill in the circle on the answer strip to show the correct word.

Sample:
    a. cheu   **b.** chooe   ⓐ ⓑ ⓒ ●
    c. chue   **d.** chew

22. **a.** peple   **b.** peaple   22. ⓐ ⓑ ⓒ ⓓ
    c. people   **d.** peopl

23. **a.** agian   **b.** again   23. ⓐ ⓑ ⓒ ⓓ
    c. agen   **d.** agin

24. **a.** tabule   **b.** tabel   24. ⓐ ⓑ ⓒ ⓓ
    c. table   **d.** tabl

25. **a.** after   **b.** ather   25. ⓐ ⓑ ⓒ ⓓ
    c. afer   **d.** aftr

26. **a.** dra   **b.** drar   26. ⓐ ⓑ ⓒ ⓓ
    c. drawe   **d.** draw

27. **a.** tried   **b.** trid   27. ⓐ ⓑ ⓒ ⓓ
    c. tride   **d.** tryed

28. **a.** litte   **b.** littel   28. ⓐ ⓑ ⓒ ⓓ
    c. little   **d.** littl

29. **a.** beatiful   **b.** beautiful   29. ⓐ ⓑ ⓒ ⓓ
    c. butiful   **d.** beutiful

30. **a.** friends   **b.** freinds   30. ⓐ ⓑ ⓒ ⓓ
    c. frends   **d.** frinds

Everyday Spelling © Scott Foresman Addison Wesley

Name _____

LESSON TEST ■ 1

■ Find the word that is spelled correctly to complete each sentence. Fill in the circle to show the correctly spelled word.

Sample:
I like to ___ the baby.
ⓐ holt   ⓑ holed
● hold   ⓓ hoold

1. It is time for ___ .
   ⓐ deb   ● bed
   ⓒ boad   ⓓ beb

2. Please ___ with me.
   ⓐ pla   ⓑ plae
   ⓒ plaee   ● play

3. We will ___ a happy song.
   ● sing   ⓑ sig
   ⓒ snig   ⓓ sng

4. I have fun at summer ___ .
   ⓐ capp   ⓑ campe
   ● camp   ⓓ cammp

5. After winter, comes ___ .
   ⓐ sprigh   ● spring
   ⓒ sring   ⓓ sping

6. He will ___ for the toy.
   ● pay   ⓑ pai
   ⓒ piae   ⓓ pauee

7. This gift is ___ you.
   ⓐ fer   ⓑ fo
   ⓒ fro   ● for

8. Put your ___ on.
   ● cap   ⓑ caap
   ⓒ cep   ⓓ caep

9. Lay it ___ on the table.
   ⓐ flaat   ⓑ flate
   ⓒ flet   ● flat

10. The new puppies are ___ .
    ⓐ fet   ⓑ faat
    ● fat   ⓓ fatt

11. Can you ___ your arm?
    ● bend   ⓑ bende
    ⓒ bened   ⓓ benned

12. An army ___ is nearby.
    ⓐ forte   ⓑ fourt
    ⓒ foret   ● fort

Name _____

2 ■ LESSON TEST

■ Find the word in each group that is spelled correctly. Fill in the circle to show the correctly spelled word.

Sample:
ⓐ sping   ⓑ sring   ● spring   ⓓ srping

1. ⓐ cood   ⓑ coud   ● could   ⓓ coud
2. ⓐ secend   ● second   ⓒ secont   ⓓ secent
3. ● kind   ⓑ cind   ⓒ cine   ⓓ kined
4. ⓐ cen   ⓑ kn   ⓒ kan   ● can
5. ⓐ sik   ⓑ sike   ● sick   ⓓ seke
6. ● woke   ⓑ wolk   ⓒ wook   ⓓ wock
7. ⓐ lik   ● like   ⓒ lk   ⓓ liek
8. ⓐ tooke   ⓑ touck   ⓒ tolk   ● took
9. ● back   ⓑ backe   ⓒ bac   ⓓ bak
10. ⓐ kik   ● kick   ⓒ kicke   ⓓ keik
11. ⓐ pak   ⓑ packe   ● pack   ⓓ pake
12. ⓐ boook   ⓑ booke   ⓒ boock   ● book

Name _____

LESSON TEST ■ 3

■ Find the word that is spelled correctly to complete each sentence. Fill in the circle to show the correctly spelled word.

Sample:
We ___ him to see Grandma.
ⓐ tolk   ● took
ⓒ tooke   ⓓ toock

1. Hit the ball with a ___ .
   ⓐ stik   ⓑ sticke
   ⓒ steck   ● stick

2. In which ___ do you live?
   ⓐ stae   ● state
   ⓒ staat   ⓓ stete

3. The apple is very ___ .
   ● sweet   ⓑ swet
   ⓒ swee   ⓓ swweet

4. Do not ___ the dish.
   ⓐ brack   ● break
   ⓒ brak   ⓓ braek

5. The leaves fell to the ___ .
   ⓐ groud   ⓑ grond
   ● ground   ⓓ grownd

6. Put the baby on the ___ .
   ⓐ swining   ⓑ swin
   ⓒ suwwing   ● swing

7. She is big and ___ .
   ⓐ breve   ⓑ bave
   ● brave   ⓓ brav

8. What a ___ idea!
   ⓐ grete   ● great
   ⓒ graet   ⓓ geat

9. I am Pedro's ___ .
   ⓐ bruther   ● brother
   ⓒ borther   ⓓ brothr

10. What ___ did you get?
    ⓐ gread   ⓑ graed
    ⓒ graid   ● grade

11. Will you please ___ up?
    ⓐ stant   ⓑ stad
    ⓒ stanted   ● stand

12. Please ___ it tomorrow.
    ● bring   ⓑ breing
    ⓒ birng   ⓓ breg

Name _____

4 ■ LESSON TEST

■ Find the word in each group that is spelled correctly. Fill in the circle to show the correctly spelled word.

Sample:
ⓐ theen   ● then   ⓒ thene   ⓓ tehn

1. ⓐ asge   ● ask   ⓒ aske   ⓓ asak
2. ⓐ diffrent   ⓑ difrent   ● different   ⓓ differnt
3. ⓐ gost   ● just   ⓒ jost   ⓓ jus
4. ● must   ⓑ musd   ⓒ mus   ⓓ musdt
5. ● desk   ⓑ deske   ⓒ desck   ⓓ desc
6. ⓐ junp   ⓑ jummp   ⓒ jupe   ● jump
7. ⓐ freind   ⓑ frend   ● friend   ⓓ firend
8. ⓐ ande   ● and   ⓒ amd   ⓓ andt
9. ⓐ wint   ● went   ⓒ whent   ⓓ wen
10. ⓐ lant   ⓑ lande   ● land   ⓓ lantd
11. ● bump   ⓑ bomp   ⓒ bup   ⓓ bumb
12. ⓐ hant   ⓑ haend   ⓒ hantd   ● hand

55

Name _____

LESSON TEST ■ 5

■ Find the word that is spelled correctly to complete each sentence. Fill in the circle to show the correctly spelled word.

Sample:
Where did ___ go?
ⓐ thay ● they
ⓒ tha ⓓ thae

1. Rain made the ___ wet.
ⓐ stretes ⓑ srtets
● streets ⓓ streats

2. I love ___ and cream.
ⓐ pechis ● peaches
ⓒ peches ⓓ petches

3. She saw ___ run to the den.
ⓐ foxs ● foxes
ⓒ fockes ⓓ foxis

4. Wash the ___.
ⓐ dishs ⓑ dishis
ⓒ dishish ● dishes

5. The shoes are in ___.
● boxes ⓑ bockes
ⓒ boxs ⓓ boxis

6. The house has six ___.
ⓐ roomes ⓑ roms
ⓒ romes ● rooms

7. The ___ are dark.
ⓐ nites ⓑ nighs
● nights ⓓ nigths

8. You can make three ___.
ⓐ whishes ⓑ wishis
● wishes ⓓ whishe

9. Your ___ are on the table.
ⓐ lunchs ⓑ lunshs
ⓒ lunshes ● lunches

10. Ten ___ are here today.
● girls ⓑ grles
ⓒ garls ⓓ grils

11. We saw ___ and tigers.
ⓐ lyens ● lions
ⓒ lons ⓓ liones

12. The ___ are playing ball.
ⓐ boyes ● boys
ⓒ boyz ⓓ boiz

5

Name _____

6A ■ REVIEW TEST

■ Find the word that is spelled correctly to complete each group of words. Fill in the circle on the answer strip to show the correct word.

Sample:
four, ___, six
a. fif   b. fiiv
c. five   d. fiv
ⓐ ⓑ ● ⓓ

1. is ___ in bed
a. sike   b. sick
c. sock   d. sik
1. ⓐ ● ⓒ ⓓ

2. girls and ___
a. boys   b. doys
c. boyz   d. boyes
2. ● ⓑ ⓒ ⓓ

3. sit at the ___
a. dask   b. desc
c. desk   d. desck
3. ⓐ ⓑ ● ⓓ

4. a ___ drawing
a. grate   b. graet
c. grat   d. great
4. ⓐ ⓑ ⓒ ●

5. ___ and tigers
a. lons   b. loins
c. lions   d. lines
5. ⓐ ⓑ ● ⓓ

6. give you three ___
a. wishes   b. whishes
c. wishis   d. wiches
6. ● ⓑ ⓒ ⓓ

7. ___ your bag
a. packe   b. pack
c. back   d. pact
7. ⓐ ● ⓒ ⓓ

6

Name _____

REVIEW TEST ■ 6B

■ Find the word that is spelled correctly to complete each group of words. Fill in the circle on the answer strip to show the correct word.

8. a ___ field
a. flat   b. flatt
c. falat   d. flate
8. ● ⓑ ⓒ ⓓ

9. she ___ come today
a. ken   b. cane
c. cen   d. can
9. ⓐ ⓑ ⓒ ●

10. her ___ and sister
a. brothe   b. bruther
c. brother   d. borther
10. ⓐ ⓑ ● ⓓ

11. candy is ___
a. sweat   b. sweet
c. swet   d. swent
11. ⓐ ● ⓒ ⓓ

12. a ___ puppy
a. fatt   b. fat
c. phat   d. fate
12. ⓐ ● ⓒ ⓓ

13. at ___ for the summer
a. cap   b. cape
c. capp   d. camp
13. ⓐ ⓑ ⓒ ●

14. a farm on the ___
a. lade   b. lad
c. land   d. lamd
14. ⓐ ⓑ ● ⓓ

7

Name _____

6C ■ REVIEW TEST

■ Find the word that is spelled correctly to complete each sentence. Fill in the circle on the answer strip to show the correct word.

Sample:
Throw the ___ into the water.
a. ston   b. stoon
c. stone   d. stown
ⓐ ⓑ ● ⓓ

15. Will you please ___ this song?
a. sing   b. sung
c. sinng   d. singing
15. ● ⓑ ⓒ ⓓ

16. This gift is ___ you.
a. fur   b. four
c. fore   d. for
16. ⓐ ⓑ ⓒ ●

17. We had fun in the snow ___.
a. forrt   b. forte
c. fort   d. fot
17. ⓐ ⓑ ● ⓓ

18. Kim ___ do it if she tried.
a. koud   b. could
c. cold   d. cood
18. ⓐ ● ⓒ ⓓ

19. Dad can sleep days or ___.
a. mights   b. nites
c. nights   d. nighs
19. ⓐ ⓑ ● ⓓ

20. She ___ I are ready to go.
a. an   b. in
c. amd   d. and
20. ⓐ ⓑ ⓒ ●

21. I ___ my new teacher.
a. like   b. lik
c. lic   d. liek
21. ● ⓑ ⓒ ⓓ

8

56

Name _____

REVIEW TEST ■ 6D

■ Find the word in each group that is spelled correctly. Fill in the circle on the answer strip to show the correct word.

Sample:
 a. gams   b. gayms   ⓐ ⓑ ⓒ ●
 c. gaymes d. games

22. a. dishish b. dishes   22. ⓐ ● ⓒ ⓓ
    c. disice   d. dishez
23. a. grownd b. groud   23. ⓐ ⓑ ● ⓓ
    c. ground   d. grond
24. a. difrent b. differnt   24. ⓐ ⓑ ● ⓓ
    c. different d. difrint
25. a. brave   b. bave   25. ● ⓑ ⓒ ⓓ
    c. brav   d. braev
26. a. secent b. secend   26. ⓐ ⓑ ⓒ ●
    c. secont   d. second
27. a. jump   b. junp   27. ● ⓑ ⓒ ⓓ
    c. jummp   d. jupe
28. a. boxez   b. boxes   28. ⓐ ● ⓒ ⓓ
    c. boxs   d. boxxes
29. a. play   b. pla   29. ● ⓑ ⓒ ⓓ
    c. plae   d. paly
30. a. baok   b. booke   30. ⓐ ⓑ ● ⓓ
    c. book   d. boock

9

Name _____

7 ■ LESSON TEST

■ Find the word that is spelled correctly to complete each sentence. Fill in the circle to show the correctly spelled word.

Sample:
 Put your ___ away.
 ⓐ stuf   ⓑ suff
 ● stuff   ⓓ stof

1. Four ___ are in the car.   7. Let us open our ___ .
   ⓐ menn   ● men   ⓐ presants ⓑ preasents
   ⓒ mene   ⓓ meen   ⓒ presints ● presents
2. I do not know ___ to go.   8. He will not cry ___ it hurts.
   ⓐ whe   ⓑ wene   ⓐ unlest   ● unless
   ⓒ whene ● when   ⓒ unles   ⓓ enless
3. He fell and hurt his ___ .   9. Mom put on her new ___ .
   ⓐ lagg   ⓑ lege   ⓐ dres   ⓑ drees
   ⓒ lage   ● leg   ● dress   ⓓ drass
4. I see ___ across the street.   10. Please, ___ me about it.
   ⓐ thim   ● them   ⓐ tel   ● tell
   ⓒ theme ⓓ tham   ⓒ tal   ⓓ thell
5. The dog's nose is ___ .   11. I am ___ a new bike.
   ● wet   ⓑ wat   ● getting ⓑ geting
   ⓒ weit   ⓓ weet   ⓒ giting ⓓ gitting
6. Please ___ me a dish.   12. He ___ his son help him.
   ⓐ git   ⓑ ge   ⓐ lat   ● let
   ● get   ⓓ gite   ⓒ leted   ⓓ lett

10

Name _____

LESSON TEST ■ 8

■ Find the word in each group that is spelled correctly. Fill in the circle to show the correctly spelled word.

Sample:
   ⓐ itto   ⓑ intoo   ● into   ⓓ itn
1. ● of   ⓑ ov   ⓒ ove   ⓓ uv
2. ⓐ clok   ● clock   ⓒ cloch   ⓓ clook
3. ⓐ sadt   ● sat   ⓒ saet   ⓓ satd
4. ⓐ tha   ⓑ thet   ● that   ⓓ thaet
5. ● rock   ⓑ rok   ⓒ rocke   ⓓ roch
6. ⓐ sadt   ⓑ saad   ⓒ satd   ● sad
7. ● doll   ⓑ dolle   ⓒ dool   ⓓ dooll
8. ⓐ jobb   ⓑ jub   ● job   ⓓ jobe
9. ● bad   ⓑ badt   ⓒ baad   ⓓ batd
10. ⓐ hav   ⓑ haf   ⓒ heve   ● have
11. ⓐ spod ⓑ spote   ● spot   ⓓ sopt
12. ⓐ vann ⓑ ven   ⓒ vanne   ● van

11

Name _____

9 ■ LESSON TEST

■ Find the word that is spelled correctly to complete each sentence. Fill in the circle to show the correctly spelled word.

Sample:
 Rabbits have cute ___ .
 ⓐ bunneys ⓑ bunnys
 ⓒ bunnis   ● bunnies

1. I will wash, ___ you dry.   7. The cat blinked ___ eye.
   ⓐ ef   ● if   ⓐ it   ⓑ its'
   ⓒ iff   ⓓ ife   ⓒ it's   ● its
2. The dog slept on the ___ .   8. Do not step into the ___ .
   ● rug   ⓑ ruge   ● mud   ⓑ mub
   ⓒ rugg   ⓓ rugge   ⓒ mude   ⓓ mudd
3. What is ___ ?   9. The chewing ___ is sweet.
   ⓐ thes   ⓑ thise   ⓐ gumb   ⓑ gome
   ⓒ theis ● this   ⓒ goom   ● gum
4. It is the right ___ to do.   10. How do those shoes ___ ?
   ⓐ thig   ● thing   ⓐ fiet   ⓑ fidd
   ⓒ theing ⓓ thaing   ● fit   ⓓ fitt
5. Jump ___ bed.   11. Please ___ the door.
   ⓐ ento   ⓑ intoo   ⓐ shud   ⓑ shutt
   ⓒ in to ● into   ● shut   ⓓ sut
6. Our class had an egg ___ .   12. Which ___ is on the rose?
   ● hunt   ⓑ hnt   ⓐ bugg   ● bug
   ⓒ hont   ⓓ hant   ⓒ buk   ⓓ bukk

12

57

Name _____

LESSON TEST ■ 10

■ Find the word in each group that is spelled correctly. Fill in the circle to show the correctly spelled word.

Sample:
● scared   (b) skerd   (c) skard   (d) scard

1. (a) luk   (b) looke   (c) loock   ● look
2. ● picked   (b) picted   (c) pickt   (d) pikt
3. (a) walkt   (b) wakled   ● walked   (d) wakked
4. (a) wot   ● want   (c) wat   (d) whant
5. (a) lookin   (b) loking   ● looking   (d) lokeing
6. (a) wonted   (b) wanted   (c) whanted   (d) whated
7. (a) cal   (b) coll   (c) cail   ● call
8. ● pick   (b) pik   (c) pic   (d) pikc
9. ● watching   (b) wacthing   (c) waching   (d) whaching
10. (a) cawling   (b) calin   (c) calind   ● calling
11. (a) wawk   (b) wauk   ● walk   (d) waak
12. ● watch   (b) wach   (c) whatch   (d) wacth

Name _____

11 ■ LESSON TEST

■ Find the word that is spelled correctly to complete each sentence. Fill in the circle to show the correctly spelled word.

Sample:
Eat an ___ in the morning.
(a) agg   (b) eagg
● egg   (d) eeg

1. I can ___ very fast.
(a) runn   (b) rn
(c) runne   ● run

2. He ___ on the rug.
(a) tript   (b) triped
● tripped   (d) tripet

3. Give me a big ___.
(a) huug   ● hug
(c) hugg   (d) hugge

4. Do not ___ that glass!
● drop   (b) dropp
(c) drup   (d) drep

5. She ___ her mom.
● hugged   (b) hagd
(c) huged   (d) hugget

6. We will go ___ in the lake.
(a) swmming   ● swimming
(c) swming   (d) swiming

7. The bluebird ___ the worm.
(a) drot   ● dropped
(c) droped   (d) dropt

8. The bus is ___ here.
(a) stoppin   (b) stupping
(c) stoping   ● stopping

9. We are back from our ___.
(a) trup   ● trip
(c) tirp   (d) tripp

10. He is ___ down the block.
(a) runing   (b) runnig
(c) runining   ● running

11. Dogs can ___ very well.
(a) swin   ● swim
(c) swimm   (d) swimme

12. Please ___ that now!
● stop   (b) stope
(c) stopp   (d) stoppe

Name _____

REVIEW TEST ■ 12A

■ Find the word that is spelled correctly to complete each group of words. Fill in the circle on the answer strip to show the correct word.

Sample:
to ___ a dish
a. brack   b. braek
c. break   d. brak
(a) (b) ● (d)

1. walking, and then ___
a. running   b. runnig
c. runing   d. rumming
1. ● (b) (c) (d)

2. took it to ___
a. then   b. tham
c. theme   d. them
2. (a) (b) (c) ●

3. ___ a hot bath
a. ge   b. get
c. gat   d. git
3. (a) ● (c) (d)

4. ___ they all come
a. when   b. wen
c. win   d. wene
4. ● (b) (c) (d)

5. ___ for my sock
a. hut   b. hont
c. hunt   d. hant
5. (a) (b) ● (d)

6. went ___ in the lake
a. swing   b. swimming
c. swmming   d. swiming
6. (a) ● (c) (d)

7. a ___ with six legs
a. bog   b. bugg
c. bug   d. bg
7. (a) (b) ● (d)

Name _____

12B ■ REVIEW TEST

■ Find the word that is spelled correctly to complete each group of words. Fill in the circle on the answer strip to show the correct word.

8. stuck in the ___
a. mub   b. mode
c. mude   d. mud
8. (a) (b) (c) ●

9. a ___ and kiss
a. hugg   b. huge
c. hug   d. hog
9. (a) (b) ● (d)

10. this one or ___ one
a. that   b. thaet
c. tat   d. thet
10. ● (b) (c) (d)

11. can't chew ___
a. gom   b. gum
c. gome   d. goom
11. (a) ● (c) (d)

12. take a ___ with her
a. wake   b. wock
c. wak   d. walk
12. (a) (b) (c) ●

13. ___ the window
a. shet   b. shout
c. shut   d. sut
13. (a) (b) ● (d)

14. ___ I like it
a. ife   b. if
c. i   d. ef
14. (a) ● (c) (d)

REVIEW TEST ■ 12C

Name _____

■ Find the word that is spelled correctly to complete each sentence. Fill in the circle on the answer strip to show the correct word.

Sample:
Come visit ___ as soon as you can.
a. jost   b. gost
c. just   d. jast
ⓐ ⓑ ● ⓓ

15. There are ants under the ___.
a. rook   b. roch
c. rack   d. rock
15. ⓐ ⓑ ⓒ ●

16. I ___ a bad cold.
a. have   b. hav
c. half   d. haf
16. ● ⓑ ⓒ ⓓ

17. We all went ___ the school.
a. in two   b. into
c. in to   d. intoo
17. ⓐ ● ⓒ ⓓ

18. Please ___ me a long story.
a. tale   b. tall
c. tell   d. till
18. ⓐ ⓑ ● ⓓ

19. I ___ the large box.
a. want   b. wont
c. what   d. whant
19. ● ⓑ ⓒ ⓓ

20. They ___ in chairs in the room.
a. saet   b. sate
c. set   d. sat
20. ⓐ ⓑ ⓒ ●

21. Last night we ___ a long way.
a. walk   b. waked
c. walkt   d. walked
21. ⓐ ⓑ ⓒ ●

12D ■ REVIEW TEST

Name _____

■ Find the word in each group that is spelled correctly. Fill in the circle on the answer strip to show the correct word.

Sample:
a. dres   b. drees
c. drass   d. dress
ⓐ ⓑ ⓒ ●

22. a. droped   b. dropped
c. dropt   d. dopped
22. ⓐ ● ⓒ ⓓ

23. a. preasents   b. presants
c. presents   d. presints
23. ⓐ ⓑ ● ⓓ

24. a. swim   b. swin
c. simm   d. swimm
24. ● ⓑ ⓒ ⓓ

25. a. geting   b. getting
c. giting   d. gitting
25. ⓐ ● ⓒ ⓓ

26. a. pick   b. pik
c. pikc   d. pic
26. ● ⓑ ⓒ ⓓ

27. a. wath   b. whatch
c. watch   d. wach
27. ⓐ ⓑ ● ⓓ

28. a. jobe   b. jub
c. jod   d. job
28. ⓐ ⓑ ⓒ ●

29. a. sopt   b. spote
c. spot   d. spott
29. ⓐ ⓑ ● ⓓ

30. a. clock   b. clook
c. cloch   d. clok
30. ● ⓑ ⓒ ⓓ

LESSON TEST ■ 13

Name _____

■ Find the word in each group that is spelled correctly. Fill in the circle to show the correctly spelled word.

Sample:
ⓐ nigths   ● nights   ⓒ nites   ⓓ nighs

1. ⓐ nexd   ● next   ⓒ nixt   ⓓ nixd
2. ⓐ livd   ⓑ livt   ⓒ leved   ● lived
3. ● across   ⓑ acros   ⓒ akross   ⓓ ackross
4. ● stayed   ⓑ stade   ⓒ staed   ⓓ stad
5. ⓐ untell   ⓑ intill   ⓒ antill   ● until
6. ⓐ allways   ● always   ⓒ all way   ⓓ alway
7. ⓐ alote   ⓑ alot   ● a lot   ⓓ alod
8. ● also   ⓑ aso   ⓒ all so   ⓓ allso
9. ⓐ apon   ⓑ opon   ● upon   ⓓ apone
10. ⓐ scard   ⓑ scaried   ● scared   ⓓ scerd
11. ● going   ⓑ goen   ⓒ goin   ⓓ gon
12. ⓐ wus   ⓑ whus   ⓒ wos   ● was

14 ■ LESSON TEST

Name _____

■ Find the word that is spelled correctly to complete each sentence. Fill in the circle to show the correctly spelled word.

Sample:
After winter, comes ___.
ⓐ sprigh   ● spring
ⓒ sring   ⓓ sping

1. We play on the same ___.
● team   ⓑ teem
ⓒ teme   ⓓ teeme

2. I saw the cat ___ its fur.
● clean   ⓑ clen
ⓒ clin   ⓓ clene

3. Wipe your ___ on the mat.
ⓐ peet   ⓑ feat
● feet   ⓓ fete

4. This year, ___ is early.
ⓐ easter   ● Easter
ⓒ Ester   ⓓ Estr

5. Please ___ this to me.
ⓐ raed   ⓑ reede
● read   ⓓ rede

6. He and I ___ have a dog.
ⓐ eatch   ⓑ eche
ⓒ ech   ● each

7. I ___ that she is here now.
ⓐ cee   ⓑ se
ⓒ scee   ● see

8. What will you ___ for lunch?
ⓐ et   ● eat
ⓒ eate   ⓓ aet

9. Can you ___ the cool rain?
● feel   ⓑ fel
ⓒ feal   ⓓ fiell

10. Brush your ___ this way.
ⓐ theeth   ⓑ teath
● teeth   ⓓ tet

11. Can you ___ a secret?
● keep   ⓑ ceep
ⓒ cep   ⓓ kep

12. Sit ___ the two of us.
ⓐ betwin   ⓑ betwen
ⓒ bettein   ● between

59

LESSON TEST ■ 15

■ Find the word in each group that is spelled correctly. Fill in the circle to show the correctly spelled word.

Sample:
● knew (b) kenew (c) neuw (d) noew

1. (a) basball (b) base ball ● baseball (d) baceball
2. ● mail (b) mael (c) mayel (d) maill
3. ● mai (b) maye (c) mye ● may
4. (a) waye ● way (c) wae (d) whae
5. (a) wate ● wait (c) waet (d) waite
6. ● take (b) taek (c) thake (d) tace
7. ● stay (b) stae (c) sta (d) stah
8. (a) rane ● rain (c) raen (d) rian
9. (a) adt (b) ait ● ate (d) aet
10. (a) paind (b) paite ● paint (d) pait
11. ● away (b) awae (c) awey (d) a waye
12. (a) macke (b) mek (c) mak ● make

16 ■ LESSON TEST

■ Find the word that is spelled correctly to complete each sentence. Fill in the circle to show the correctly spelled word.

Sample:
The ___ are wet with rain.
(a) stretes ● streets
(c) streats (d) srtets

1. I can ___ you a trick.
   (a) showe (b) seou
   (c) sowe ● show
2. We live ___ on a hill.
   (a) hight (b) hie
   ● high (d) hiy
3. Step into the ___ slowly.
   (a) bote (b) boute
   ● boat (d) baot
4. Do your work the ___ way.
   ● right (b) righth
   (c) ritte (d) rihgt
5. I do not ___ if you do not.
   (a) minde (b) miad
   (c) minte ● mind
6. Will you ___ me the ball?
   (a) trow ● throw
   (c) traw (d) thro
7. My duck can ___ in the tub.
   (a) floote ● float
   (c) flaut (d) floot
8. I saw a ___ on the farm.
   ● goat (b) goot
   (c) gaot (d) gote
9. Turn on the ___ please.
   (a) lith (b) lihgt
   ● light (d) ligth
10. This is my ___ pencil.
    (a) owen (b) owne
    (c) oun ● own
11. Can you ___ where I hid it?
    (a) finde ● find
    (c) feind (d) fiend
12. We all go home at ___.
    (a) nighe (b) nite
    (c) nigth ● night

LESSON TEST ■ 17

■ Find the word in each group that is spelled correctly. Fill in the circle to show the correctly spelled word.

Sample:
(a) lunshes (b) lunchs ● lunches (d) lunshs

1. (a) teu ● too (c) towe (d) towo
2. ● chew (b) cheu (c) chue (d) chooe
3. ● room (b) rume (c) roun (d) romme
4. (a) mon ● moon (c) mone (d) meun
5. (a) fod (b) fode (c) fowd ● food
6. ● new (b) nue (c) newe (d) nuw
7. (a) gorwed (b) groo (c) gru ● grew
8. (a) zeu (b) zew ● zoo (d) zo
9. (a) blogh (b) blu ● blew (d) bloew
10. (a) sone ● soon (c) seun (d) soone
11. (a) fluew (b) flwe (c) fliw ● flew
12. ● knew (b) kenew (c) noew (d) neuw

18A ■ REVIEW TEST

■ Find the group of words in which the underlined word is misspelled. Fill in the circle on the answer strip to show that group of words.

Sample:
a. leaves on the tree
b. a graet big kiss
c. when the bus comes
d. a sweet, juicy apple
(a) ● (c) (d)

1. a. open or shut
   b. letters and other mayel
   c. the best thing to do
   d. across the wide street
   1. (a) ● (c) (d)
2. a. swims like a fish
   b. between you and me
   c. the rite thing to do
   d. to follow the leader
   2. (a) (b) ● (d)
3. a. flat on his back
   b. looked at the clock
   c. flue the kite today
   d. sat on the ground
   3. (a) (b) ● (d)
4. a. to ship the big boxes
   b. take it away from here
   c. big bump on the head
   d. allways do a good job
   4. (a) (b) (c) ●
5. a. red me the book
   b. my brother and sister
   c. a truck or a van
   d. the families are going
   5. ● (b) (c) (d)
6. a. a bend in the road
   b. livd on a little farm
   c. camping out at night
   d. will check the papers
   6. (a) ● (c) (d)
7. a. sat on wet paite
   b. to push the cart
   c. not much money
   d. getting ready to go
   7. ● (b) (c) (d)

Name _____

REVIEW TEST ■ 18B

■ Find the group of words in which the underlined word is misspelled. Fill in the circle on the answer strip to show that group of words.

8. a. played with the boys
   b. mud on our shoes
   c. trip on the old rug
   d. on the teem that won

   8. ⓐ ⓑ ⓒ ●

9. a. aet a big meal
   b. did not fit well
   c. grew a few inches
   d. swimming very far

   9. ● ⓑ ⓒ ⓓ

10. a. running up the road
    b. dropped in the snow
    c. will leave very son
    d. a Halloween party

    10. ⓐ ⓑ ● ⓓ

11. a. will go my way
    b. fowd on the table
    c. because they want
    d. have a green car

    11. ⓐ ● ⓒ ⓓ

12. a. dishes in the sink
    b. blew a large bubble
    c. a clock with no hands
    d. no shoes on her feat

    12. ⓐ ⓑ ⓒ ●

13. a. clean, white teeth
    b. a bout on the lake
    c. ride three ponies
    d. hugged her child

    13. ⓐ ● ⓒ ⓓ

14. a. mak a large box
    b. out in the rain
    c. until the next day
    d. a stick of gum

    14. ● ⓑ ⓒ ⓓ

Name _____

18C ■ REVIEW TEST

■ Find the word that is spelled correctly to complete each sentence. Fill in the circle on the answer strip to show the correct word.

Sample:
We were ___ TV.
a. waching   b. whaching
c. watching   d. wacthing

ⓐ ⓑ ● ⓓ

15. I have a ___ toy.
    a. now   b. mew
    c. new   d. knew

    15. ⓐ ⓑ ● ⓓ

16. Please ___ me the ball.
    a. thore   b. thow
    c. through   d. throw

    16. ⓐ ⓑ ⓒ ●

17. The jet is ___ in the air.
    a. hie   b. hight
    c. hi   d. high

    17. ⓐ ⓑ ⓒ ●

18. I like you ___.
    a. a lot   b. allot
    c. alot   d. alote

    18. ● ⓑ ⓒ ⓓ

19. Did you ___ your pencil?
    a. fied   b. fined
    c. find   d. finde

    19. ⓐ ⓑ ● ⓓ

20. You can ___ how cold my hands are.
    a. feal   b. feel
    c. fell   d. fill

    20. ⓐ ● ⓒ ⓓ

21. She has made up her ___ to go.
    a. mide   b. mine
    c. mind   d. minde

    21. ⓐ ⓑ ● ⓓ

Name _____

REVIEW TEST ■ 18D

■ Find the word in each group that is spelled correctly. Fill in the circle on the answer strip to show the correct word.

Sample:
a. ef   b. iff
c. ife   d. if

ⓐ ⓑ ⓒ ●

22. a. scared   b. scard
    c. skerd   d. skard

    22. ● ⓑ ⓒ ⓓ

23. a. a pone   b. apon
    c. opon   d. upon

    23. ⓐ ⓑ ⓒ ●

24. a. basball b. baceball
    c. baseball d. base ball

    24. ⓐ ⓑ ● ⓓ

25. a. stay   b. sta
    c. saty   d. stae

    25. ● ⓑ ⓒ ⓓ

26. a. cep   b. keep
    c. kep   d. ceep

    26. ⓐ ● ⓒ ⓓ

27. a. ech   b. each
    c. eatch   d. eche

    27. ⓐ ● ⓒ ⓓ

28. a. mun   b. muon
    c. mone   d. moon

    28. ⓐ ⓑ ⓒ ●

29. a. gowing   b. goning
    c. going   d. goin

    29. ⓐ ⓑ ● ⓓ

30. a. was   b. wase
    c. wus   d. wos

    30. ● ⓑ ⓒ ⓓ

Name _____

19 ■ LESSON TEST

■ Find the word in each group that is spelled correctly. Fill in the circle to show the correctly spelled word.

Sample:
ⓐ wat   ⓑ wate   ⓒ wath   ● what

1. ⓐ happe   ● happy   ⓒ hapey   ⓓ happey
2. ⓐ pritty   ● pretty   ⓒ prity   ⓓ prety
3. ⓐ eg   ⓑ eeg   ● egg   ⓓ agg
4. ● tall   ⓑ tawl   ⓒ tal   ⓓ taul
5. ⓐ betur   ● better   ⓒ beder   ⓓ beter
6. ⓐ ful   ⓑ foll   ⓒ fole   ● full
7. ⓐ cary   ● carry   ⓒ carrye   ⓓ carrey
8. ● follow   ⓑ follo   ⓒ folow   ⓓ folo
9. ● stuff   ⓑ stuf   ⓒ stof   ⓓ stofe
10. ⓐ halloween ⓑ holloween ● Halloween ⓓ hallween
11. ⓐ wil   ⓑ wel   ⓒ whill   ● will
12. ⓐ atd   ⓑ att   ● add   ⓓ adt

Name _____

LESSON TEST ■ 20

■ Find the word that is spelled correctly to complete each sentence. Fill in the circle to show the correctly spelled word.

Sample:
Did you ___ the glass?
(a) brack (b) braek
(c) brak ● break

1. Button your ___.
   ● shirt (b) shert
   (c) shrit (d) shurt

2. That ___ is broken.
   (a) chare (b) chir
   ● chair (d) chiar

3. Where is ___ cat?
   (a) tha ● the
   (c) teh (d) th

4. Are ___ too many?
   (a) thar (b) thair
   (c) thier ● there

5. I know ___ I will do.
   (a) waht (b) wat
   (c) wut ● what

6. He will ___ his work.
   (a) cheack ● check
   (c) chec (d) chech

7. Please finish, ___ clean up.
   ● then (b) thene
   (c) tehn (d) theen

8. I wonder ___ Mom went.
   (a) wer (b) whare
   ● where (d) wher

9. The dog is brown and ___.
   ● white (b) wite
   (c) wight (d) whit

10. We must ___ the package.
    (a) shep ● ship
    (c) shipp (d) shipe

11. What a good ___ she is!
    ● child (b) chid
    (c) childe (d) ciled

12. We will eat when ___ arrive.
    (a) thay (b) tha
    (c) thae ● they

Name _____

21 ■ LESSON TEST

■ Find the word in each group that is spelled correctly. Fill in the circle to show the correctly spelled word.

Sample:
(a) aske (b) asge ● ask (d) asak

1. ● bath (b) baath (c) batth (d) bothe
2. (a) warsh (b) waush ● wash (d) wost
3. (a) wich ● which (c) whitch (d) wicth
4. ● inch (b) intch (c) ench (d) insh
5. ● crash (b) crach (c) cratsh (d) chrash
6. (a) cach ● catch (c) cacth (d) cech
7. (a) whith (b) weth ● with (d) wiht
8. (a) puch (b) pusch (c) puhs ● push
9. (a) mutch ● much (c) moch (d) musch
10. ● reach (b) reech (c) reesh (d) reatch
11. (a) bolth (b) bouth (c) bothe ● both
12. (a) pich ● pitch (c) pictch (d) pithch

Name _____

LESSON TEST ■ 22

■ Find the word that is spelled correctly to complete each sentence. Fill in the circle to show the correctly spelled word.

Sample:
She has a wonderful ___.
(a) frend ● friend
(c) frind (d) freind

1. The ___ has a new colt.
   ● horse (b) hores
   (c) hourse (d) hors

2. Which of ___ is yours?
   (a) thos ● those
   (c) thoes (d) thoses

3. The park is a pretty ___.
   (a) plase (b) plas
   (c) plaes ● place

4. Do ___ belong to her?
   ● these (b) thes
   (c) theese (d) thees

5. It is very ___ of you.
   (a) nis (b) nic
   (c) nise ● nice

6. Will you ___ help?
   (a) plese ● please
   (c) pleas (d) ples

7. We live in a brick ___.
   (a) hows ● house
   (c) houes (d) hous

8. He swims ___ a week.
   (a) wuns (b) onec
   ● once (d) wonce

9. It is ___ it is hot.
   (a) becouse (b) becuse
   (c) becase ● because

10. She hopes to win the ___.
    (a) ras ● race
    (c) raes (d) rase

11. Can you ___ this crayon?
    (a) yoos (b) uooz
    ● use (d) uese

12. I hear ___ music.
    (a) dans (b) dace
    (c) danc ● dance

Name _____

23 ■ LESSON TEST

■ Find the word in each group that is spelled correctly. Fill in the circle to show the correctly spelled word.

Sample:
(a) thim ● them (c) tham (d) thum

1. (a) poney ● pony (c) ponie (d) ponny
2. ● baby (b) babay (c) babey (d) babby
3. (a) storyies (b) storys (c) stroys ● stories
4. ● family (b) famly (c) faimly (d) famaly
5. (a) pupes ● puppies (c) pupies (d) puppys
6. (a) babys ● babies (c) babyes (d) babbies
7. (a) pupy (b) pupey ● puppy (d) puppie
8. (a) poneys (b) ponys (c) ponneys ● ponies
9. (a) bunneys ● bunnies (c) bunnys (d) bunnis
10. ● families (b) familys (c) famlies (d) familyes
11. (a) storey (b) storie ● story (d) storee
12. ● bunny (b) bunee (c) buny (d) bunney

Name _____

REVIEW TEST ■ 24A

■ Find the group of words in which the underlined word is misspelled. Fill in the circle on the answer strip to show that group of words.

Sample:
a. could not see it
b. to asge for help
c. days and nights
d. wishes for a dog

ⓐ ● ⓒ ⓓ

1. a. cap on his head
   b. dishes on the table
   c. went to a show
   d. wight sheet of paper

1. ⓐ ⓑ ⓒ ●

2. a. went there ounce
   b. to put into boxes
   c. bump on his leg
   d. to play the game

2. ● ⓑ ⓒ ⓓ

3. a. took a walk
   b. to pay for the toy
   c. sit on a char
   d. pack of wolves

3. ⓐ ⓑ ● ⓓ

4. a. marks an ench apart
   b. brother and sister
   c. to sing a song
   d. will jump up and down

4. ● ⓑ ⓒ ⓓ

5. a. pages in a book
   b. take a hot bathe
   c. must come home now
   d. different from this one

5. ⓐ ● ⓒ ⓓ

6. a. in your desk
   b. my home state
   c. are thay coming
   d. to land on the floor

6. ⓐ ⓑ ● ⓓ

7. a. go to the dance
   b. lions and tigers
   c. to add and subtract
   d. a loud chrash outside

7. ⓐ ⓑ ⓒ ●

Name _____

24B ■ REVIEW TEST

■ Find the group of words in which the underlined word is misspelled. Fill in the circle on the answer strip to show that group of words.

8. a. for you and me
   b. two ripe apples
   c. ducks and bunnys
   d. add these up

8. ⓐ ⓑ ● ⓓ

9. a. to bend down
   b. follo a girl in front
   c. just like you
   d. three nights ago

9. ⓐ ● ⓒ ⓓ

10. a. will carry it for you
    b. to reach up for it
    c. has a good use
    d. cheack all his work

10. ⓐ ⓑ ⓒ ●

11. a. six in my famly
    b. a good book
    c. a spot on his car
    d. to kick it hard

11. ● ⓑ ⓒ ⓓ

12. a. each of they books
    b. to swing back and forth
    c. stand next to
    d. down on hard ground

12. ● ⓑ ⓒ ⓓ

13. a. to let him go
    b. to catch a fish
    c. mother, father, and ciled
    d. play in a fort

13. ⓐ ⓑ ● ⓓ

14. a. give you three wishes
    b. boys in a game
    c. has been very sick
    d. hear storys at bedtime

14. ⓐ ⓑ ⓒ ●

Name _____

REVIEW TEST ■ 24C

■ Find the word that is spelled correctly to complete each sentence. Fill in the circle on the answer strip to show the correct word.

Sample:
Do not be late for ___.
a. skule   b. skule
c. school   d. sckool

ⓐ ⓑ ● ⓓ

15. Don't ___ a lot of water.
    a. uese   b. use
    c. us   d. yous

15. ⓐ ● ⓒ ⓓ

16. This is too ___ for me.
    a. much   b. mach
    c. moch   d. mush

16. ● ⓑ ⓒ ⓓ

17. My grandfather lives in a big ___.
    a. hose   b. house
    c. hous   d. houes

17. ⓐ ● ⓒ ⓓ

18. Do you see the ___ on the lake?
    a. seep   b. shipe
    c. sip   d. ship

18. ⓐ ⓑ ⓒ ●

19. She will take the can ___ her.
    a. weth   b. whith
    c. with   d. whit

19. ⓐ ⓑ ● ⓓ

20. The man likes to ride his ___.
    a. horse   b. hoarse
    c. hourse   d. hores

20. ● ⓑ ⓒ ⓓ

21. We just got a new ___.
    a. puppey   b. puppy
    c. pupy   d. puppie

21. ⓐ ● ⓒ ⓓ

Name _____

24D ■ REVIEW TEST

■ Find the word in each group that is spelled correctly. Fill in the circle on the answer strip to show the correct word.

Sample:
a. steck   b. stik
c. stic   d. stick

ⓐ ⓑ ⓒ ●

22. a. holloween   b. Halloween
    c. halloween   d. Hollaween

22. ⓐ ● ⓒ ⓓ

23. a. ponies   b. ponys
    c. ponees   d. ponyies

23. ● ⓑ ⓒ ⓓ

24. a. shert   b. shurt
    c. shrit   d. shirt

24. ⓐ ⓑ ⓒ ●

25. a. prety   b. pretty
    c. prity   d. pritty

25. ⓐ ● ⓒ ⓓ

26. a. becouse   b. becaus
    c. because   d. becuse

26. ⓐ ⓑ ● ⓓ

27. a. stuff   b. stuf
    c. stof   d. stofe

27. ● ⓑ ⓒ ⓓ

28. a. egg   b. agg
    c. eagg   d. eeg

28. ● ⓑ ⓒ ⓓ

29. a. bouth   b. both
    c. borth   d. bothe

29. ⓐ ● ⓒ ⓓ

30. a. ras   b. rase
    c. race   d. raes

30. ⓐ ⓑ ● ⓓ

LESSON TEST ■ 25

■ Find the word that is spelled correctly to complete each sentence. Fill in the circle to show the correctly spelled word.

Sample:
If you need help, ___ on me.
(a) cal (b) coll
● call (d) coil

1. I ___ like to go sledding.
● would (b) woud
(c) wold (d) whould

2. Pick ___ of the best ones.
(a) som (b) sume
● some (d) sone

3. I hope ___ child will help.
(a) evey (b) evry
(c) avre ● every

4. Are you ___ tired?
(a) realy (b) relly
(c) rilly ● really

5. Mom will ___ me supper.
(a) giv ● give
(c) gev (d) geve

6. He is a ___ happy puppy.
(a) verry (b) verey
(c) varee ● very

7. Is that ___ house?
(a) their (b) ther
(c) thar (d) thiar

8. Light is coming ___ the glass.
● through (b) thrugh
(c) throgh (d) thrwe

9. Have ___ done your work?
(a) yo (b) yow
● you (d) ya

10. The ___ show is great!
(a) wole ● whole
(c) whol (d) hoil

11. Think ___ you speak.
(a) beefor (b) befor
(c) befour ● before

12. What is your ___ song?
(a) favrit (b) favrite
● favorite (d) favorit

26 ■ LESSON TEST

■ Find the word in each group that is spelled correctly. Fill in the circle to show the correctly spelled word.

Sample:
(a) pithch (b) pictch (c) pich ● pitch

1. (a) toun (b) twon ● town (d) tonw
2. ● about (b) abot (c) a bout (d) abowt
3. (a) aut ● out (c) ot (d) owt
4. (a) owr (b) ar (c) oure ● our
5. (a) nauw (b) naw ● now (d) noe
6. ● found (b) founed (c) fownd (d) founde
7. (a) maus ● mouse (c) mause (d) mous
8. (a) doun ● down (c) daun (d) downe
9. (a) roud (b) rownd (c) roand ● round
10. (a) hou (b) haw (c) howe ● how
11. (a) klown ● clown (c) klaun (d) claun
12. ● sound (b) sond (c) sownd (d) sowd

LESSON TEST ■ 27

■ Find the word that is spelled correctly to complete each sentence. Fill in the circle to show the correctly spelled word.

Sample:
I once rode a big ___.
● horse (b) hores
(c) hors (d) hourse

1. How ___ away do you live?
(a) fure (b) farre
(c) firr ● far

2. It is ___ to learn to swim.
(a) hord ● hard
(c) harb (d) harde

3. We had a ___ for Dad.
(a) pardy ● party
(c) partey (d) partty

4. His dog has a loud ___.
● bark (b) barck
(c) brck (d) brok

5. It gets ___ after 5:00.
(a) darke (b) drack
● dark (d) darck

6. I would like to visit a ___.
(a) farn (b) fram
(c) furm ● farm

7. Pull your sister in the ___.
(a) carte (b) crt
● cart (d) carde

8. We saw the band ___.
(a) mardsh (b) mardch
(c) martch ● march

9. She has a cut on her ___.
(a) aurt ● arm
(c) aerm (d) aurm

10. What ___ do you play?
● part (b) prt
(c) purt (d) parte

11. The cows are in the ___.
● barn (b) barne
(c) barrn (d) brn

12. We ___ without you.
(a) strated (b) starded
● started (d) startid

28 ■ LESSON TEST

■ Find the word in each group that is spelled correctly. Fill in the circle to show the correctly spelled word.

Sample:
● lion (b) lyon (c) leon (d) lyen

1. ● first (b) frist (c) ferst (d) firt
2. (a) bern (b) birn (c) burne ● burn
3. (a) hert ● hurt (c) hirt (d) herte
4. (a) lern ● learn (c) learne (d) larn
5. (a) prson (b) prsen ● person (d) persen
6. (a) garl (b) grle (c) gril ● girl
7. (a) har ● her (c) hre (d) hr
8. ● were (b) weare (c) woer (d) wer
9. (a) turne (b) tirn (c) tirne ● turn
10. (a) haerd (b) hurd (c) heerd ● heard
11. (a) turtel ● turtle (c) trutle (d) turttl
12. ● bird (b) burd (c) bured (d) bired

Name _____

LESSON TEST ■ 29

■ Find the word that is spelled correctly to complete each sentence. Fill in the circle to show the correctly spelled word.

Sample:
May I have ___ one more?
ⓐ jost   ⓑ gost
ⓒ jus   ● just

1. I can do it ___ myself.
   ⓐ bey   ⓑ bie
   ⓒ biy   ● by

2. We are all ___ now.
   ⓐ hir   ⓑ herre
   ● here   ⓓ heare

3. He has gone ___ see her.
   ⓐ towe   ⓑ tu
   ● to   ⓓ ta

4. Do you ___ the way?
   ● know   ⓑ nowe
   ⓒ noew   ⓓ noo

5. Close one ___ at a time.
   ⓐ eey   ● eye
   ⓒ ei   ⓓ eaye

6. Our ___ cousins are here.
   ⓐ tuo   ● two
   ⓒ tu   ⓓ taw

7. At last, I have ___!
   ⓐ wone   ⓑ wun
   ● won   ⓓ whon

8. Do you ___ the music?
   ⓐ heer   ⓑ heare
   ⓒ hir   ● hear

9. I think Mom said ___.
   ⓐ noo   ⓑ mo
   ● no   ⓓ nao

10. ___ think it is Tuesday.
    ⓐ Y   ● I
    ⓒ Ey   ⓓ i

11. I would like to ___ a book.
    ● buy   ⓑ bey
    ⓒ bai   ⓓ bie

12. Which ___ would you like?
    ⓐ wun   ● one
    ⓒ whone   ⓓ wan

41

Name _____

30A ■ REVIEW TEST

■ Find the word that is spelled correctly to complete each group of words. Fill in the circle on the answer strip to show the correct word.

Sample:
___ up at 7 o'clock
a. whok   b. wook
c. woke   d. wock

ⓐ ⓑ ● ⓓ

1. ___ thing or another
   a. wone   b. on
   c. one   d. won

   1. ⓐ ⓑ ● ⓓ

2. a ___ dark sky
   a. very   b. vary
   c. verry   d. vere

   2. ● ⓑ ⓒ ⓓ

3. saw it ___ the window
   a. trough   b. threw
   c. throw   d. through

   3. ⓐ ⓑ ⓒ ●

4. people in the ___
   a. twon   b. town
   c. ton   d. toun

   4. ⓐ ● ⓒ ⓓ

5. showed her ___ to ride the bike
   a. how   b. haw
   c. hou   d. who

   5. ● ⓑ ⓒ ⓓ

6. money to ___ the food
   a. bey   b. by
   c. buy   d. bye

   6. ⓐ ⓑ ● ⓓ

7. get there ___ I do
   a. be for   b. befour
   c. befor   d. before

   7. ⓐ ⓑ ⓒ ●

42

Name _____

REVIEW TEST ■ 30B

■ Find the word that is spelled correctly to complete each group of words. Fill in the circle on the answer strip to show the correct word.

8. fell ___ on the rug
   a. doun   b. down
   c. bown   d. don

   8. ⓐ ● ⓒ ⓓ

9. rock ___ the tall tree
   a. dy   b. by
   c. buy   d. biy

   9. ⓐ ● ⓒ ⓓ

10. ___ or three children
    a. two   b. to
    c. too   d. tow

    10. ● ⓑ ⓒ ⓓ

11. took the ___ bag
    a. wole   b. holl
    c. hole   d. whole

    11. ⓐ ⓑ ⓒ ●

12. felt the ___ bump
    a. hrd   b. heard
    c. hard   d. hod

    12. ⓐ ⓑ ● ⓓ

13. ___ how to do it
    a. know   b. kow
    c. no   d. now

    13. ● ⓑ ⓒ ⓓ

14. team ___ the big game
    a. one   b. won
    c. wun   d. wone

    14. ⓐ ● ⓒ ⓓ

43

Name _____

30C ■ REVIEW TEST

■ Find the word that is spelled correctly to complete each sentence. Fill in the circle on the answer strip to show the correct word.

Sample:
Tell him ___ one you want.
a. wich   b. whitch
c. which   d. wiche

ⓐ ⓑ ● ⓓ

15. Please come ___ my magic show.
    a. tow   b. too
    c. two   d. to

    15. ⓐ ⓑ ⓒ ●

16. Every child has a ___ in the play.
    a. part   b. port
    c. prt   d. prat

    16. ● ⓑ ⓒ ⓓ

17. I need ___ paper.
    a. som   b. same
    c. some   d. sum

    17. ⓐ ⓑ ● ⓓ

18. She can tell that you ___ late.
    a. were   b. wher
    c. where   d. wer

    18. ● ⓑ ⓒ ⓓ

19. I ___ like a fresh orange.
    a. woud   b. wold
    c. would   d. wood

    19. ⓐ ⓑ ● ⓓ

20. He ___ to race fast.
    a. stated   b. started
    c. starded   d. stared

    20. ⓐ ● ⓒ ⓓ

21. You will get ___ more candy!
    a. on   b. now
    c. know   d. no

    21. ⓐ ⓑ ⓒ ●

44

Name _____

REVIEW TEST ■ 30D

■ Find the word in each group that is spelled correctly. Fill in the circle on the answer strip to show the correct word.

Sample:
a. acros   b. acrost
c. accross   d. across   ⓐ ⓑ ⓒ ●

22. a. favorite   b. favrit
    c. favrite   d. favorit   22. ● ⓑ ⓒ ⓓ
23. a. prson   b. peson
    c. persen   d. person   23. ⓐ ⓑ ⓒ ●
24. a. owt   b. aut
    c. out   d. ot   24. ⓐ ⓑ ● ⓓ
25. a. a bout   b. abot
    c. abowt   d. about   25. ⓐ ⓑ ⓒ ●
26. a. sowd   b. sound
    c. sownd   d. sond   26. ⓐ ● ⓒ ⓓ
27. a. bark   b. berk
    c. brok   d. barck   27. ● ⓑ ⓒ ⓓ
28. a. ya   b. you
    c. u   d. yo   28. ⓐ ● ⓒ ⓓ
29. a. frst   b. firt
    c. frist   d. first   29. ⓐ ⓑ ⓒ ●
30. a. evrey   b. evry
    c. every   d. evey   30. ⓐ ⓑ ● ⓓ

Name _____

31 ■ LESSON TEST

■ Find the word in each group that is spelled correctly. Fill in the circle to show the correctly spelled word.

Sample:
ⓐ gote   ⓑ gaot   ⓒ goot   ● goat

1. ⓐ some thing   ● something   ⓒ somthing   ⓓ somting
2. ⓐ birtday   ● birthday   ⓒ birth day   ⓓ berthday
3. ⓐ bathtup   ⓑ bafftub   ⓒ bathtube   ● bathtub
4. ⓐ somthines   ⓑ somtimes   ● sometimes   ⓓ some times
5. ⓐ air plane   ● airplane   ⓒ airplain   ⓓ ariplane
6. ⓐ everthing   ● everything   ⓒ every thing   ⓓ evrething
7. ● outside   ⓑ outsied   ⓒ out sid   ⓓ out side
8. ● everybody   ⓑ eavrybody   ⓒ every body   ⓓ everbody
9. ⓐ sun chine   ⓑ sonshine   ● sunshine   ⓓ sun shin
10. ● playground   ⓑ play ground   ⓒ playgrownd   ⓓ playgrowd
11. ⓐ my self   ⓑ myselfe   ● myself   ⓓ myslef
12. ● inside   ⓑ insid   ⓒ in cide   ⓓ innside

Name _____

LESSON TEST ■ 32

■ Find the word that is spelled correctly to complete each sentence. Fill in the circle to show the correctly spelled word.

Sample:
I like to ___ TV at 7:00.
ⓐ wach   ● watch
ⓒ wacth   ⓓ whatch

1. He thought I ___ see him.
   ⓐ din't   ● didn't
   ⓒ dident   ⓓ didnt
2. Why ___ he home yet?
   ⓐ isnt   ⓑ is'nt
   ⓒ isen't   ● isn't
3. Mom said ___ one for you.
   ⓐ ders   ● there's
   ⓒ thers   ⓓ ther's
4. Oh, ___ the one I wanted!
   ● here's   ⓑ heares
   ⓒ heres   ⓓ heers
5. I think ___ mine.
   ⓐ thats   ⓑ thatts
   ● that's   ⓓ thas
6. Do you know if ___ ready?
   ⓐ its   ⓑ itss
   ● it's   ⓓ i'ts
7. I hope ___ not the last one.
   ⓐ Im   ⓑ i'm
   ⓒ Ime   ● I'm
8. I ___ want to do that.
   ● don't   ⓑ downt
   ⓒ dont   ⓓ dount
9. They said ___ ready to start.
   ⓐ ther   ⓑ thar
   ⓒ the're   ● they're
10. Are you sure you ___ do it?
    ⓐ con't   ● can't
    ⓒ kant   ⓓ cant
11. She ___ the first to finish.
    ⓐ wasen't   ● wasn't
    ⓒ wasent   ⓓ was'nt
12. Now ___ on our way.
    ⓐ wer   ⓑ weer
    ● we're   ⓓ we'r

Name _____

33 ■ LESSON TEST

■ Find the word in each group that is spelled correctly. Fill in the circle to show the correctly spelled word.

Sample:
ⓐ realy   ⓑ relly   ● really   ⓓ rilly

1. ● crawl   ⓑ craul   ⓒ crael   ⓓ crawal
2. ⓐ smal   ⓑ smol   ⓒ samll   ● small
3. ⓐ hawl   ⓑ haule   ● hall   ⓓ halle
4. ⓐ aweful   ⓑ awfull   ● awful   ⓓ aful
5. ⓐ bole   ● ball   ⓒ bawle   ⓓ bal
6. ● fall   ⓑ fawl   ⓒ fal   ⓓ flol
7. ⓐ bougth   ⓑ bot   ⓒ boaught   ● bought
8. ⓐ brouth   ⓑ brot   ● brought   ⓓ broght
9. ● saw   ⓑ sall   ⓒ sawe   ⓓ sowe
10. ⓐ ole   ⓑ al   ⓒ ol   ● all
11. ⓐ thout   ● thought   ⓒ thot   ⓓ thaught
12. ⓐ drawe   ● draw   ⓒ dra   ⓓ dray

Name _____

LESSON TEST ■ 3

■ Find the word that is spelled correctly to complete each sentence. Fill in the circle to show the correctly spelled word.

Sample:
We ___ him to see Grandma.
- ⓐ tolk
- ● took
- ⓒ tooke
- ⓓ toock

1. Hit the ball with a ___ .
   - ⓐ stik
   - ⓑ sticke
   - ⓒ steck
   - ⓓ stick

2. In which ___ do you live?
   - ⓐ stae
   - ⓑ state
   - ⓒ staat
   - ⓓ stete

3. The apple is very ___ .
   - ⓐ sweet
   - ⓑ swet
   - ⓒ swee
   - ⓓ swweet

4. Do not ___ the dish.
   - ⓐ brack
   - ⓑ break
   - ⓒ brak
   - ⓓ braek

5. The leaves fell to the ___ .
   - ⓐ groud
   - ⓑ grond
   - ⓒ ground
   - ⓓ grownd

6. Put the baby on the ___ .
   - ⓐ swining
   - ⓑ swin
   - ⓒ suwwing
   - ⓓ swing

7. She is big and ___ .
   - ⓐ breve
   - ⓑ bave
   - ⓒ brave
   - ⓓ brav

8. What a ___ idea!
   - ⓐ great
   - ⓑ grat
   - ⓒ graet
   - ⓓ geat

9. I am Pedro's ___ .
   - ⓐ bruther
   - ⓑ brother
   - ⓒ borther
   - ⓓ brothr

10. What ___ did you get?
    - ⓐ gread
    - ⓑ graed
    - ⓒ graid
    - ⓓ grade

11. Will you please ___ up?
    - ⓐ stant
    - ⓑ stad
    - ⓒ stanted
    - ⓓ stand

12. Please ___ it tomorrow.
    - ⓐ bring
    - ⓑ breing
    - ⓒ birng
    - ⓓ breg

Name _____

4 ■ LESSON TEST

■ Find the word in each group that is spelled correctly. Fill in the circle to show the correctly spelled word.

Sample:
   ⓐ theen   ● then   ⓒ thene   ⓓ tehn

1. ⓐ asge   ⓑ ask   ⓒ aske   ⓓ asak

2. ⓐ difrent   ⓑ difrent   ⓒ different   ⓓ differnt

3. ⓐ gost   ⓑ just   ⓒ jost   ⓓ jus

4. ⓐ must   ⓑ musd   ⓒ mus   ⓓ musdt

5. ⓐ desk   ⓑ deske   ⓒ desck   ⓓ desc

6. ⓐ junp   ⓑ jummp   ⓒ jupe   ⓓ jump

7. ⓐ freind   ⓑ frend   ⓒ friend   ⓓ firend

8. ⓐ ande   ⓑ and   ⓒ amd   ⓓ andt

9. ⓐ wint   ⓑ went   ⓒ whent   ⓓ wen

10. ⓐ lant   ⓑ lande   ⓒ land   ⓓ lantd

11. ⓐ bump   ⓑ bomp   ⓒ bup   ⓓ bumb

12. ⓐ hant   ⓑ haend   ⓒ hantd   ⓓ hand

Everyday Spelling © Scott Foresman Addison Wesley

Name _____

LESSON TEST ■ 5

■ Find the word that is spelled correctly to complete each sentence. Fill in the circle to show the correctly spelled word.

Sample:
Where did ___ go?
(a.) thay   ● they
(c.) tha   (d.) thae

1. Rain made the ___ wet.
   (a.) stretes   (b.) srtets
   (c.) streets   (d.) streats

2. I love ___ and cream.
   (a.) pechis   (b.) peaches
   (c.) peches   (d.) petches

3. She saw ___ run to the den.
   (a.) foxs   (b.) foxes
   (c.) fockes   (d.) foxis

4. Wash the ___ .
   (a.) dishs   (b.) dishis
   (c.) dishish   (d.) dishes

5. The shoes are in ___ .
   (a.) boxes   (b.) bockes
   (c.) boxs   (d.) boxis

6. The house has six ___ .
   (a.) roomes   (b.) roms
   (c.) romes   (d.) rooms

7. The ___ are dark.
   (a.) nites   (b.) nighs
   (c.) nights   (d.) nigths

8. You can make three ___ .
   (a.) whishes   (b.) wishis
   (c.) wishes   (d.) whishe

9. Your ___ are on the table.
   (a.) lunchs   (b.) lunshs
   (c.) lunshes   (d.) lunches

10. Ten ___ are here today.
    (a.) girls   (b.) grles
    (c.) garls   (d.) grils

11. We saw ___ and tigers.
    (a.) lyens   (b.) lions
    (c.) lons   (d.) liones

12. The ___ are playing ball.
    (a.) boyes   (b.) boys
    (c.) boyz   (d.) boiz

Name _____

LESSON TEST ■ 13

■ Find the word in each group that is spelled correctly. Fill in the circle to show the correctly spelled word.

Sample:
  (a) nigths   ● nights   (c) nites   (d) nighs

1. (a) nexd   (b) next   (c) nixt   (d) nixd
2. (a) livd   (b) livt   (c) leved   (d) lived
3. (a) across (b) acros   (c) akross (d) ackross
4. (a) stayed (b) stade   (c) staed   (d) stad
5. (a) untell (b) intill   (c) antill (d) until
6. (a) allways (b) always   (c) all way (d) alway
7. (a) alote   (b) alot   (c) a lot   (d) alod
8. (a) also   (b) aso   (c) all so (d) allso
9. (a) apon   (b) opon   (c) upon   (d) apone
10. (a) scard (b) scaried (c) scared (d) scerd
11. (a) going (b) goen   (c) goin   (d) gon
12. (a) wus   (b) whus   (c) wos   (d) was

Name _____

14 ■ LESSON TEST

■ Find the word that is spelled correctly to complete each sentence. Fill in the circle to show the correctly spelled word.

Sample:
After winter, comes ____ .
ⓐ sprigh   ● spring
ⓒ sring   ⓓ sping

1. We play on the same ____ .
   ⓐ team   ⓑ teem
   ⓒ teme   ⓓ teeme

2. I saw the cat ____ its fur.
   ⓐ clean   ⓑ clen
   ⓒ clin   ⓓ clene

3. Wipe your ____ on the mat.
   ⓐ peet   ⓑ feat
   ⓒ feet   ⓓ fete

4. This year, ____ is early.
   ⓐ easter ⓑ Easter
   ⓒ Ester   ⓓ Estr

5. Please ____ this to me.
   ⓐ raed   ⓑ reede
   ⓒ read   ⓓ rede

6. He and I ____ have a dog.
   ⓐ eatch   ⓑ eche
   ⓒ ech   ⓓ each

7. I ____ that she is here now.
   ⓐ cee   ⓑ se
   ⓒ scee   ⓓ see

8. What will you ____ for lunch?
   ⓐ et   ⓑ eat
   ⓒ eate   ⓓ aet

9. Can you ____ the cool rain?
   ⓐ feel   ⓑ fel
   ⓒ feal   ⓓ fiell

10. Brush your ____ this way.
    ⓐ theeth ⓑ teath
    ⓒ teeth   ⓓ tet

11. Can you ____ a secret?
    ⓐ keep   ⓑ ceep
    ⓒ cep   ⓓ kep

12. Sit ____ the two of us.
    ⓐ betwin ⓑ betwen
    ⓒ bettein ⓓ between

Everyday Spelling © Scott Foresman Addison Wesley

Name _____

LESSON TEST ■ 15

■ Find the word in each group that is spelled correctly. Fill in the circle to show the correctly spelled word.

Sample:
- ● knew   ○ b) kenew   ○ c) neuw   ○ d) noew

1. a) basball   b) base ball   c) baseball   d) baceball
2. a) mail   b) mael   c) mayel   d) maill
3. a) mai   b) maye   c) mye   d) may
4. a) waye   b) way   c) wae   d) whae
5. a) wate   b) wait   c) waet   d) waite
6. a) take   b) taek   c) thake   d) tace
7. a) stay   b) stae   c) sta   d) stah
8. a) rane   b) rain   c) raen   d) rian
9. a) adt   b) ait   c) ate   d) aet
10. a) paind   b) paite   c) paint   d) pait
11. a) away   b) awae   c) awey   d) a waye
12. a) macke   b) mek   c) mak   d) make

Everyday Spelling © Scott Foresman Addison Wesley

21

Name _____

REVIEW TEST ■ 24C

■ Find the word that is spelled correctly to complete each sentence. Fill in the circle on the answer strip to show the correct word.

Sample:
Do not be late for ___.
a. skool   b. skule
c. school   d. sckool

ⓐ ⓑ ● ⓓ

15. Don't ___ a lot of water.
    a. uese   b. use
    c. us   d. yous

15. ⓐ ⓑ ⓒ ⓓ

16. This is too ___ for me.
    a. much   b. mach
    c. moch   d. mush

16. ⓐ ⓑ ⓒ ⓓ

17. My grandfather lives in a big ___.
    a. hose   b. house
    c. hous   d. houes

17. ⓐ ⓑ ⓒ ⓓ

18. Do you see the ___ on the lake?
    a. seep   b. shipe
    c. sip   d. ship

18. ⓐ ⓑ ⓒ ⓓ

19. She will take the can ___ her.
    a. weth   b. whith
    c. with   d. whit

19. ⓐ ⓑ ⓒ ⓓ

20. The man likes to ride his ___.
    a. horse   b. hoarse
    c. hourse   d. hores

20. ⓐ ⓑ ⓒ ⓓ

21. We just got a new ___.
    a. puppey   b. puppy
    c. pupy   d. puppie

21. ⓐ ⓑ ⓒ ⓓ

Name _____

24D ■ REVIEW TEST

■ Find the word in each group that is spelled correctly. Fill in the circle on the answer strip to show the correct word.

Sample:
    a. steck   b. stik   ⓐ ⓑ ⓒ ●
    c. stic   d. stick

22. a. holloween   b. Halloween   22. ⓐ ⓑ ⓒ ⓓ
    c. halloween   d. Hollaween

23. a. ponies   b. ponys   23. ⓐ ⓑ ⓒ ⓓ
    c. ponees   d. ponyies

24. a. shert   b. shurt   24. ⓐ ⓑ ⓒ ⓓ
    c. shrit   d. shirt

25. a. prety   b. pretty   25. ⓐ ⓑ ⓒ ⓓ
    c. prity   d. pritty

26. a. becouse   b. becaus   26. ⓐ ⓑ ⓒ ⓓ
    c. because   d. becuse

27. a. stuff   b. stuf   27. ⓐ ⓑ ⓒ ⓓ
    c. stof   d. stofe

28. a. egg   b. agg   28. ⓐ ⓑ ⓒ ⓓ
    c. eagg   d. eeg

29. a. bouth   b. both   29. ⓐ ⓑ ⓒ ⓓ
    c. borth   d. bothe

30. a. ras   b. rase   30. ⓐ ⓑ ⓒ ⓓ
    c. race   d. raes

Name _____

LESSON TEST ■ 25

■ Find the word that is spelled correctly to complete each sentence. Fill in the circle to show the correctly spelled word.

Sample:
If you need help, ____ on me.
a. cal   b. coll
● call   d. coil

1. I ____ like to go sledding.
   a. would   b. woud
   c. wold   d. whould

2. Pick ____ of the best ones.
   a. som   b. sume
   c. some   d. sone

3. I hope ____ child will help.
   a. evey   b. evry
   c. avre   d. every

4. Are you ____ tired?
   a. realy   b. relly
   c. rilly   d. really

5. Mom will ____ me supper.
   a. giv   b. give
   c. gev   d. geve

6. He is a ____ happy puppy.
   a. verry   b. verey
   c. varee   d. very

7. Is that ____ house?
   a. their   b. ther
   c. thar   d. thiar

8. Light is coming ____ the glass.
   a. through   b. thrugh
   c. throgh   d. thrwe

9. Have ____ done your work?
   a. yo   b. yow
   c. you   d. ya

10. The ____ show is great!
    a. wole   b. whole
    c. whol   d. hoil

11. Think ____ you speak.
    a. beefor   b. befor
    c. befour   d. before

12. What is your ____ song?
    a. favrit   b. favrite
    c. favorite d. favorit

Everyday Spelling © Scott Foresman Addison Wesley

Name _____

REVIEW TEST ■ 36A

■ Find the group of words in which the underlined word is misspelled. Fill in the circle on the answer strip to show that group of words.

Sample:
   a. <u>next</u> one to go
   b. <u>grue</u> so fast
   c. <u>blew</u> a big bubble
   d. visit the <u>zoo</u>

ⓐ ● ⓒ ⓓ

1. a. <u>throw</u> it to me
   b. <u>here's</u> the best one
   c. <u>don't</u> know what to do
   d. went in an <u>air plane</u>

1. ⓐ ⓑ ⓒ ⓓ

2. a. she <u>also</u> came
   b. <u>cought</u> the fast dog
   c. a very <u>happy</u> puppy
   d. once <u>upon</u> a time

2. ⓐ ⓑ ⓒ ⓓ

3. a. <u>cann't</u> see the spot
   b. once <u>lived</u> with us
   c. <u>didn't</u> want to go
   d. was <u>always</u> smiling

3. ⓐ ⓑ ⓒ ⓓ

4. a. <u>comes</u> on the bus
   b. <u>gos</u> to my school
   c. on our large <u>farm</u>
   d. laid an <u>egg</u>

4. ⓐ ⓑ ⓒ ⓓ

5. a. like the show <u>a lot</u>
   b. see the <u>baseball</u> game
   c. going <u>out side</u> to play
   d. take the <u>other</u> one

5. ⓐ ⓑ ⓒ ⓓ

6. a. <u>there's</u> a new one
   b. <u>puppies</u> and kittens
   c. a very pretty <u>flowr</u>
   d. <u>until</u> he is asleep

6. ⓐ ⓑ ⓒ ⓓ

7. a. <u>siad</u> to the man
   b. <u>small</u> toy for her
   c. on a losing <u>team</u>
   d. fall off the <u>desk</u>

7. ⓐ ⓑ ⓒ ⓓ

Name _____

36B ■ REVIEW TEST

■ Find the group of words in which the underlined word is misspelled. Fill in the circle on the answer strip to show that group of words.

8. a. <u>ate</u> a ripe, red apple
    b. a <u>bright</u> green car
    c. look <u>over</u> there
    d. <u>thout</u> about swimming

    8. ⓐ ⓑ ⓒ ⓓ

9. a. <u>running</u> to the store
    b. like being in the <u>sun shine</u>
    c. eat some French <u>fries</u>
    d. <u>he's</u> not coming

    9. ⓐ ⓑ ⓒ ⓓ

10. a. the <u>right</u> thing to do
    b. has on a <u>watch</u>
    c. for her <u>brithday</u> party
    d. got a <u>Christmas</u> card

    10. ⓐ ⓑ ⓒ ⓓ

11. a. I <u>want</u> you here
    b. <u>take</u> this with you
    c. do it <u>once</u> more
    d. <u>dont</u> have a pencil

    11. ⓐ ⓑ ⓒ ⓓ

12. a. a bat and a <u>bole</u>
    b. a bug under a <u>rock</u>
    c. our two <u>families</u>
    d. a lot of <u>presents</u>

    12. ⓐ ⓑ ⓒ ⓓ

13. a. started a <u>new</u> job
    b. look at the <u>clock</u>
    c. <u>a nother</u> week to go
    d. <u>something</u> is on fire

    13. ⓐ ⓑ ⓒ ⓓ

14. a. hands are not <u>clean</u>
    b. even if <u>were</u> not going
    c. get in the <u>bathtub</u>
    d. <u>plant</u> it over there

    14. ⓐ ⓑ ⓒ ⓓ

Name _____

REVIEW TEST ■ 36C

■ Find the word that is spelled correctly to complete each sentence. Fill in the circle on the answer strip to show the correct word.

Sample:
Come and ___ with me.
a. tak   b. tawk
c. talk   d. take

ⓐ ⓑ ● ⓓ

15. Do you think ___ coming?
    a. Im   b. i'm
    c. I'm   d. I'am

    15. ⓐ ⓑ ⓒ ⓓ

16. The class went out to the ___.
    a. play ground   b. play grond
    c. playgrownd   d. playground

    16. ⓐ ⓑ ⓒ ⓓ

17. We ___ him when he jumped up.
    a. saw   b. so
    c. sall   d. sow

    17. ⓐ ⓑ ⓒ ⓓ

18. He ___ very sad about the news.
    a. wasen't   b. wasn't
    c. wasnt   d. wasent

    18. ⓐ ⓑ ⓒ ⓓ

19. We had to stay ___ because of rain.
    a. in sid   b. insid
    c. in side   d. inside

    19. ⓐ ⓑ ⓒ ⓓ

20. We ___ eggs and bread at the store.
    a. bot   b. bout
    c. bote   d. bought

    20. ⓐ ⓑ ⓒ ⓓ

21. He did ___ he could to help his mother.
    a. everything   b. everthing
    c. evrything   d. every thing

    21. ⓐ ⓑ ⓒ ⓓ

Name _____

LESSON TEST ■ 34

■ Find the word that is spelled correctly to complete each sentence. Fill in the circle to show the correctly spelled word.

Sample:
The boys ____ home together.
● went   ⓑ wint
ⓒ whent ⓓ wen

1. Do you have a ____ crayon?
   ● purple   ⓑ perple
   ⓒ purpl   ⓓ purpul

2. Pick a shirt of ____ color.
   ⓐ a nother   ⓑ anouther
   ● another   ⓓ anather

3. I bit into a sweet ____ .
   ⓐ appel   ⓑ appl
   ● apple   ⓓ appal

4. She brushes ____ eating.
   ⓐ afther   ⓑ afeter
   ⓒ aftr   ● after

5. Will he ____ get here?
   ⓐ evere   ● ever
   ⓒ aver   ⓓ evr

6. The glass rolled off the ____ .
   ⓐ tabel   ● table
   ⓒ tabble   ⓓ tabule

7. There are 30 ____ in here.
   ⓐ peaple   ⓑ peple
   ● people   ⓓ peapul

8. Should I do it ____ again?
   ● over   ⓑ ovre
   ⓒ ovr   ⓓ overe

9. What is ____ your chair?
   ⓐ ander   ⓑ undere
   ⓒ onder   ● under

10. It's a pretty ____ song.
    ⓐ littel   ⓑ litte
    ● little   ⓓ littl

11. Take one or the ____ .
    ● other   ⓑ ather
    ⓒ outher   ⓓ otheer

12. Put the ____ into the vase.
    ⓐ flowr   ⓑ flowre
    ⓒ flawr   ● flower

Name _____

35 ■ LESSON TEST

■ Find the word in each group that is spelled correctly. Fill in the circle to show the correctly spelled word.

Sample:
● march   ⓑ martch   ⓒ mardch   ⓓ mardsh

1. ● tried   ⓑ tride   ⓒ treid   ⓓ tryed
2. ⓐ specil   ● special   ⓒ speical   ⓓ speshel
3. ⓐ gouse   ⓑ gose   ● goes   ⓓ gos
4. ⓐ agen   ⓑ agin   ● again   ⓓ agian
5. ⓐ cildren ⓑ chillren ⓒ childeren ● children
6. ⓐ ho   ● who   ⓒ whoe   ⓓ whoo
7. ● said   ⓑ sead   ⓒ siad   ⓓ sed
8. ⓐ caht   ● caught   ⓒ cought   ⓓ cauht
9. ⓐ frends   ● friends   ⓒ freinds   ⓓ frens
10. ⓐ beatiful ⓑ beautifull ⓒ beutiful ● beautiful
11. ⓐ aint   ⓑ ont   ● aunt   ⓓ awnt
12. ⓐ Chrishmas ⓑ christmas ⓒ Chrismas ● Christmas

Name _____

REVIEW TEST ■ 36A

■ Find the group of words in which the underlined word is misspelled. Fill in the circle on the answer strip to show that group of words.

Sample:
 a. next one to go
 b. grue so fast
 c. blew a big bubble
 d. visit the zoo
ⓐ ● ⓒ ⓓ

1. a. throw it to me
   b. here's the best one
   c. don't know what to do
   d. went in an air plane
   1. ⓐ ⓑ ⓒ ●

2. a. she also came
   b. cought the fast dog
   c. a very happy puppy
   d. once upon a time
   2. ⓐ ● ⓒ ⓓ

3. a. cann't see the spot
   b. once lived with us
   c. didn't want to go
   d. was always smiling
   3. ● ⓑ ⓒ ⓓ

4. a. comes on the bus
   b. gos to my school
   c. on our large farm
   d. laid an egg
   4. ⓐ ● ⓒ ⓓ

5. a. like the show a lot
   b. see the baseball game
   c. going out side to play
   d. take the other one
   5. ⓐ ⓑ ● ⓓ

6. a. there's a new one
   b. puppies and kittens
   c. a very pretty flowr
   d. until he is asleep
   6. ⓐ ⓑ ● ⓓ

7. a. siad to the man
   b. small toy for her
   c. on a losing team
   d. fall off the desk
   7. ● ⓑ ⓒ ⓓ

Name _____

36B ■ REVIEW TEST

■ Find the group of words in which the underlined word is misspelled. Fill in the circle on the answer strip to show that group of words.

8. a. ate a ripe, red apple
   b. a bright green car
   c. look over there
   d. thout about swimming
   8. ⓐ ⓑ ⓒ ●

9. a. running to the store
   b. like being in the sun shine
   c. eat some French fries
   d. he's not coming
   9. ⓐ ● ⓒ ⓓ

10. a. the right thing to do
    b. has on a watch
    c. for her brithday party
    d. got a Christmas card
    10. ⓐ ⓑ ● ⓓ

11. a. I want you here
    b. take this with you
    c. do it once more
    d. dont have a pencil
    11. ⓐ ⓑ ⓒ ●

12. a. a bat and a bole
    b. a bug under a rock
    c. our two families
    d. a lot of presents
    12. ● ⓑ ⓒ ⓓ

13. a. started a new job
    b. look at the clock
    c. a nother week to go
    d. something is on fire
    13. ⓐ ⓑ ● ⓓ

14. a. hands are not clean
    b. even if were not going
    c. get in the bathtub
    d. plant it over there
    14. ⓐ ● ⓒ ⓓ

Name _____

REVIEW TEST ■ 36C

■ Find the word that is spelled correctly to complete each sentence. Fill in the circle on the answer strip to show the correct word.

Sample:
Come and ___ with me.
a. tak   b. tawk
c. talk   d. take   ⓐ ⓑ ● ⓓ

15. Do you think ___ coming?
    a. Im   b. i'm
    c. I'm   d. I'am   15. ⓐ ⓑ ● ⓓ

16. The class went out to the ___.
    a. play ground   b. play grond
    c. playgrownd   d. playground 16. ⓐ ⓑ ⓒ ●

17. We ___ him when he jumped up.
    a. saw   b. so
    c. sall   d. sow   17. ● ⓑ ⓒ ⓓ

18. He ___ very sad about the news.
    a. wasen't   b. wasn't
    c. wasnt   d. wasent   18. ⓐ ● ⓒ ⓓ

19. We had to stay ___ because of rain.
    a. in sid   b. insid
    c. in side   d. inside   19. ⓐ ⓑ ⓒ ●

20. We ___ eggs and bread at the store.
    a. bot   b. bout
    c. bote   d. bought   20. ⓐ ⓑ ⓒ ●

21. He did ___ he could to help his mother.
    a. everything   b. everthing
    c. evrything   d. every thing 21. ● ⓑ ⓒ ⓓ

53

Name _____

36D ■ REVIEW TEST

■ Find the word in each group that is spelled correctly. Fill in the circle on the answer strip to show the correct word.

Sample:
a. cheu   b. chooe
c. chue   d. chew   ⓐ ⓑ ⓒ ●

22. a. peple   b. peaple
    c. people   d. peopl   22. ⓐ ⓑ ● ⓓ

23. a. agian   b. again
    c. agen   d. agin   23. ⓐ ● ⓒ ⓓ

24. a. tabule   b. tabel
    c. table   d. tabl   24. ⓐ ⓑ ● ⓓ

25. a. after   b. ather
    c. afer   d. aftr   25. ● ⓑ ⓒ ⓓ

26. a. dra   b. drar
    c. drawe   d. draw   26. ⓐ ⓑ ⓒ ●

27. a. tried   b. trid
    c. tride   d. tryed   27. ● ⓑ ⓒ ⓓ

28. a. litte   b. littel
    c. little   d. littl   28. ⓐ ⓑ ● ⓓ

29. a. beatiful   b. beautiful
    c. butiful   d. beutiful   29. ⓐ ● ⓒ ⓓ

30. a. friends   b. freinds
    c. frends   d. frinds   30. ● ⓑ ⓒ ⓓ

54